THE SABBATH

Other Books by the Author

An Historical and Geographical Study Guide of Israel

~

A Passover Haggadah for Jewish Believers

~

Biblical Lovemaking: A Study of the Song of Solomon

~

Commentary Series: The Book of Genesis

~

Commentary Series: Judges and Ruth

~

Commentary Series: The Messianic Jewish Epistles

~

God's Will, Man's Will

~

Israeolology: The Missing Link in Systematic Theology Messianic Christology

~

Jesus Was A Jew

~

*The Footsteps of the Messiah:
A Study of the Sequence of Prophetic Events*

~

*The Remnant of Israel: The History, Theology, and Philosophy
of the Messianic Community*

THE SABBATH

ARNOLD G. FRUCHTENBAUM
TH.M., PH.D.

אריאל ARIEL
MINISTRIES

© 2012 by Arnold G. Fruchtenbaum, Th.M., Ph.D.
2nd Edition 2014
ISBN: 978-1-935174-41-7

Published by Ariel Ministries
P.O. Box 792507
San Antonio, TX 78279-2507
www.ariel.org

ISBN: 978-1-935174-21-9 (pbk) (2012)
ISBN: 978-1-935174-22-6 (ebook)

Library of Congress Control Number:
2012950254

REL101000 RELIGION / Messianic Judaism

All rights reserved. No part of this manuscript may be reproduced in any form, except in brief quotations in a review or professional work, without permission from the publishers.

All Scripture quotations, unless otherwise noted, are from the *1901 American Standard Version* (Oak Harbor, WA: Logos Research Systems, Inc., 1994). However, the archaic language has been changed with one exception: The archaic *ye* has been retained in order to distinguish the second person plural from the singular *you*. Also *Christ* has been replaced with the word *Messiah*, and *Jesus* has been changed to His Hebrew name, *Yeshua*.

Printed in the United States of America

Cover illustration by Jesse Gonzales (*http://www.vipgraphics.net*)

Published by

ARIEL MINISTRIES

The Work is Dedicated to

Jacques and Sharon Gabizon

For Their Excellent Work

In Establishing

Ariel Canada

CONTENTS

I. INTRODUCTION AND DEFINITION 1

A. Introduction 1

B. Definition of the Word 1

II. THE SABBATH IN JUDAISM 3

A. The Concepts of the Sabbath 3

B. The Personifications of the Sabbath 4

C. The Laws of the Sabbath 4

D. The Essential Elements for Sabbath 5
   1. Sabbath Foods 5
   2. Sabbath Lights 6
   3. Sabbath Wine 7

E. The Meals of the Sabbath 8

III. THE SABBATH IN GENESIS 9

A. The Exposition 9

B. The Issue 9

C. Summary 13

IV. THE SABBATH IN THE LAW OF MOSES 15

A. The Passages 15
   1. Exodus 16:23-30 15
   2. Exodus 20:8-11 16
   3. Exodus 23:12 17

4. Exodus 31:12-17	18
5. Exodus 34:21	19
6. Exodus 35:1-3	19
7. Leviticus 16:31	19
8. Leviticus 19:3	20
9. Leviticus 19:30	20
10. Leviticus 23:3	20
11. Leviticus 23:11	21
12. Leviticus 23:15-16	21
13. Leviticus 23:32	21
14. Leviticus 23:38	22
15. Leviticus 24:5-9	22
16. Leviticus 26:2	22
17. Numbers 15:32-36	22
18. Numbers 28:9-10	23
19. Deuteronomy 5:12-15	23
B. The Sabbath Commandment Proper	**25**
1. The Inconsistencies	25
2. The Misapplications	26
C. The Sabbath as a Sign	**32**
D. The Ceremonial Aspects of the Sabbath	**33**
E. The Features of the Sabbath	**33**
F. The Perpetuity of the Sabbath	**35**
1. The Basis	35
2. Application and Conclusion	37
G. The Law of Moses Rendered Inoperative	**38**
1. The First Eight Passages	38
a. Romans 7:1-6	38
b. Romans 10:4	39
c. Galatians 3:19a	39
d. Galatians 3:24-25	39
e. Ephesians 2:11-16	40
f. Hebrews 7:11-12, and 18	40
g. Hebrews 8:13	41
h. II Corinthians 3:2-11	41
2. Summary and Conclusions	42
3. The Ninth Passage: Matthew 5:17-19	42

H. The Ceremonial, Civil, and Moral Distinctions   43

I. The Moral Law and the Law of Moses   46

J. Is the Sabbath Law Moral or Ceremonial?   47

K. Conclusion   48

V. THE SABBATH IN THE PROPHETS   51

A. The Passages   51
1. II Kings 4:23   51
2. II Kings 11:5, 7, and 9   51
3. II Kings 16:18   52
4. Isaiah 1:13   52
5. Isaiah 56:1-8   52
6. Isaiah 58:13   53
7. Isaiah 66:23   53
8. Jeremiah 17:21-27   54
9. Ezekiel 20:12-24   55
10. Ezekiel 22:8   56
11. Ezekiel 22:26   56
12. Ezekiel 23:38   56
13. Ezekiel 44:24   57
14. Ezekiel 45:17   57
15. Ezekiel 46:1-5   57
16. Ezekiel 46:12   58
17. Hosea 2:11   59
18. Amos 8:5   59

B. Observations and Conclusions   59

VI. THE SABBATH IN THE WRITINGS   61

A. Key Passages   61
1. I Chronicles 9:32   61
2. I Chronicles 23:31   61
4. II Chronicles 8:13   62
5. II Chronicles 31:2-3   62
6. Nehemiah 9:14   63

7. Nehemiah 10:31	63
8. Nehemiah 10:33	63
9. Nehemiah 13:15-22	64
10. Psalm 92: Superscription	65
11. Lamentations 1:7	66
12. Lamentations 2:6	66
B. Observations and Conclusions	**66**

VII. THE SABBATH IN THE NEW TESTAMENT 69

A. The Sabbath in the Gospels   **69**
  1. The Sabbath Events   71
    a. The First Visit to Nazareth   71
    b. Authority over Demons   71
    c. The Healing of the Paralytic   72
    d. The Controversy over the Grain   79
    e. The Healing of the Man with the Withered Hand   82
    f. The Second Visit to Nazareth   84
    g. Sabbath Healing and the Keeping of the Law   85
    h. The Healing of a Man Born Blind   85
    i. The Healing of the Crippled Woman   86
    j. The Healing of the Man with Dropsy   87
    k. The Sabbath in the Great Tribulation   88
    l. The Sabbath and the Death and Burial of the Messiah   88
    m. The Sabbath Visit to the Tomb   89
  2. Observations and Conclusions   90
    a. The Areas of Conflict   90
    b. The Sabbath in Rabbinic Judaism   90
    c. Yeshua's Interpretation of the Sabbath   90
    d. No Mandate for Sabbath-Keeping   91

B. The Sabbath in the Book of Acts   **92**
  1. The Sabbath Passages   92
  2. Observations   92
  3. Jewish Believers in the Synagogue   93
  4. Two Relevant Passages   94
    a. Acts 15:1-20   94
    b. Acts 21:20-24   95
  5. Conclusion   96

C. The Sabbath in the Epistles of Paul 96
 1. The Passages 96
  a. Colossians 2:16-17 96
  b. Romans 14:4-6a 97
  c. Galatians 4:10 98
 2. Conclusion 98

D. The Sabbath in the Book of Hebrews 99
 1. The Two Passages 99
 2. The Typology of the Sabbath 100

E. Summary and Conclusions 101

VIII. THE ISSUE OF SUNDAY 103

A. The Origin of Sunday Observance 103
 1. The Misconception 103
 2. The Origin of the Sunday Sabbath 103
 3. The Beginning of the Sunday Service 106
 4. The Basis of Sunday Worship 107
 5. The Evidence from the *Talmud* 107

B. The First Day of the Week 108
 1. The Names 108
 2. The Lord's Day 108
 3. Acts 20:7-8 and 11 108
 4. Not Obligatory as a Day of Worship 112
 5. The Status of Sunday 112
 6. The Freedom to Choose 112
 7. The Conclusion 113

IX. THE SABBATH AND SUNDAY: SUMMARY AND CONCLUSIONS 115

X. THE SABBATICAL YEAR 117

A. The Passages 117
 1. Exodus 23:10-11 117
 2. Leviticus 25:1-7 117

3. Leviticus 25:18-22   118
4. Leviticus 26:34-35 and 43a   119
5. Deuteronomy 15:1-11   120
6. Deuteronomy 31:9-13   121
7. II Chronicles 36:21b   121
8. Nehemiah 8:18   121
9. Nehemiah 10:31   122

B. Observations and Conclusions   122

C. The Names   123

D. The Biblical Laws   123

E. Rabbinic Laws and Traditions   124

F. The Ramifications   125

G. The History of its Observance   126

XI. THE YEAR OF JUBILEE   127

A. The Passages   127
  1. Leviticus 25:8-55   127
    a. Leviticus 25:8-12   127
    b. Leviticus 25:13-17   128
    c. Leviticus 25:18-22   129
    d. Leviticus 25:23-28   129
    e. Leviticus 25:29-34   129
    f. Leviticus 25:35-38   130
    g. Leviticus 25:39-46   130
    h. Leviticus 25:47-55   130
  3. Numbers 36:4   132
  4. Isaiah 61:2   132
  5. Ezekiel 46:17   133
  6. Observations and Conclusions   133

B. The Names   134

C. The Biblical Laws   135

D. Rabbinic Laws and Traditions   136

E. The Ramifications 136

F. The History of its Observance 138

XII. THE PRINCIPLE OF FREEDOM 139

SCRIPTURE INDEX 141

BIBLIOGRAPHY 147

I. INTRODUCTION AND DEFINITION

A. Introduction

This is a somewhat detailed study on the Sabbath because there is so much confusion among both Jewish believers and Gentile believers about what the Bible really teaches concerning the Sabbath.

In Pharisaic Judaism, which developed after the Babylonian Captivity and was thriving during the time when *Yeshua* walked the earth, the Sabbath became a major observance to the point that it was personified as the Bride of Israel and as Jehovah's Queen. When the question was raised, "Why did God create Israel?" the answer was, "God made Israel to honor the Sabbath." Therefore, Israel was made for the Sabbath. In the centuries to come, this teaching became the basis of all different schools of Judaism. Understandably, Jewish believers today are still struggling with the question of what to do with the Sabbath.

Gentile believers too, mostly due to the lack of studying the Scriptures with the proper understanding of their Jewish roots, ponder the question of what they should do with the Sabbath. Are they to keep it? Did Sunday replace it? When are believers to corporately worship the Lord?

The purpose of this study, then, will be to examine what the Sabbath is in both Testaments. At the same time, it will try to examine arguments used to support mandatory Sabbath-keeping.

B. Definition of the Word

The English word "Sabbath" comes from the Hebrew word *shabbat*. This word is used in multiple ways in the Hebrew Bible. The verbal form is used 71 times in various contexts to signify something ceasing (Joshua 5:12; Isaiah 24:8; Nehemiah 6:3) or being completely absent (Lamentations 5:14; Ezekiel 6:6). It also has imbedded within it the concept of judgment as God promises to put an end to the wicked (Isaiah 13:11; Hosea 1:4). However, the noun form is of primary interest for the topic at hand and, used 111 times in the Scriptures, usually signifies the weekly day of rest. The double b in *shabbat* has an intensive force, implying a complete cessation from work. Based on its relation to the verbal form, this noun indicates a complete cessation of work (Exodus 20:10). The notion of Sabbath in the Mosaic Law is rooted in the creation account of Genesis. Just as God rested after creating, so Jews are commanded to rest as well (Exodus 20:11). This day is to be revered by the children of Israel (Exodus 20:8).

So the root meaning of the word Sabbath is "to desist," "to cease," "to rest." As a name for the day of the week, it is unique in the Hebrew Old Testament in that it is the only day that is actually named. The English language gives names to all seven days of the week: Sunday, Monday, Tuesday, Wednesday, Thursday, Friday, and Saturday. However, in the Hebrew tongue, both ancient and modern, the Sabbath, the seventh day of the week, is the only day that is named. All the other days are numbered. For example, Sunday is "day one," Monday is "day two," Tuesday is "day three," Wednesday is "day four," Thursday is "day five," and Friday is "day six." However, Saturday is referred to both as "day seven" in Genesis 2 and as the Sabbath day beginning with the Law of Moses.

II. THE SABBATH IN JUDAISM

Judaism has made a great deal out of the Sabbath. Before A.D. 70, the Temple was the most important element in Judaism, but once the Temple was destroyed, the Sabbath took priority. It is not the purpose of this study to mention everything that Judaism has done with the Sabbath. Rather, we will focus on the main features so as to understand both the Jewish observance of the Sabbath today and also to better understand why there was so much conflict between *Yeshua* (Jesus) and the Pharisees over the proper way of observing the Sabbath.

A. The Concepts of the Sabbath

The major concept of the Sabbath in Judaism is that of *menuchah*, the Hebrew word for "rest." The concept of *menuchah* in Judaism includes the rest of the body, the mind, and the spirit. On this day, work is banished and replaced by *menuchah*: rest.

There are many minor concepts involved in the Sabbath. One is the fact that the Sabbath is a time for the study of the *Torah* (Law). Another minor concept is that it is a time for family companionship. It also serves as a weekly protest against slavery, since slaves had to work all seven days of the week. According to Orthodox Judaism, it is on this day that Jews receive an additional soul for the Sabbath. Furthermore, the Sabbath is a foundation of the faith. It is the Sabbath that gave rise to synagogues. The Sabbath is associated with personal salvation, because it is a foretaste of the bliss stored up for the righteous in the world to come.

According to Judaism, the Sabbath has three age-long functions. First, it enables one to devote himself fully, one day of the week, to the task of becoming "a kingdom of priests and a holy nation" and, in that way, beautifying one's life. Second, it prevents one from becoming enslaved to secular activities, showing freedom from enslavement to Egypt. And third, it proves one's trust in God: that He will provide even without the material gain of working on the Sabbath.

B. The Personifications of the Sabbath

Judaism has personified the Sabbath in three ways. The Sabbath is seen as a "bride," emphasizing the loveliness of the Sabbath. On Friday night, the Jewish people receive the Sabbath Bride with hymns. The famous, 3rd century Rabbi Hanina said that on the eve of the Sabbath we should say, "Come, let us go out to meet the Bride, the Queen." Another famous rabbi, Rabbi Jannai, would cry as the Sabbath was coming in, "Come, oh Bride! Come, oh Bride!"[1]

A second way the Sabbath is personified is as a "queen," emphasizing the graciousness of the Sabbath. On Friday afternoon, the mystics of the town of Safed in Israel used to go out into the fields outside the city to receive Queen Sabbath. Lastly, the Sabbath is seen as a "princess," emphasizing its charm.

C. The Laws of the Sabbath

Altogether the rabbis came up with about one thousand five hundred different rules and regulations concerning the Sabbath. These were derived from thirty-nine areas of work which were forbidden on the Sabbath day.

These thirty-nine areas were based on the construction of the Tabernacle in the wilderness. The rabbis arrived at their deduction in this manner: The Scripture passage on constructing the Tabernacle and the passage prohibiting work on the Sabbath were put side by side. This juxtaposition of the passages was interpreted as meaning that no work was allowed on the Tabernacle on the Sabbath day. Therefore, the prohibited work for the Sabbath day was in whatever area of work that was required for the Tabernacle. The rabbis concluded that there were thirty-nine areas of work on the Tabernacle which were forbidden on the Sabbath day.

---

[1] *B. Shabbat* 119a: "R. Hanina robed himself and stood at sunset of Sabbath eve [and] exclaimed, 'Come and let us go forth to welcome the queen Sabbath.'(2) R. Jannai donned his robes, on Sabbath eve and exclaimed, 'Come, O bride, Come, O bride!'"

These original thirty-nine areas of work were known as *avot*, a Hebrew word meaning "fathers." The *avot* work or the "fathers' work" was the actual work on the Tabernacle itself that was forbidden on the Sabbath day.

From these thirty-nine areas the rabbis developed many *toldot*, a Hebrew word meaning "offspring" or "derivatives." They decided which other works man does that would fit into these areas. These were other labors in the same area that shared a common purpose with the *avot* works. Therefore, they were also forbidden.

Through a form of rabbinic logic known as *pilpul*, the rabbis derived many new rules and regulations out of the original thirty-nine areas of work forbidden on the Tabernacle on the Sabbath day. By the time all of the laws were developed, there were approximately one thousand five hundred rules and regulations for the Sabbath day. These are largely still followed in Orthodox Judaism today.

D. The Essential Elements for Sabbath

There are three basic essentials for Sabbath observance: first, *challah*, an egg-bread whose yellow color is due to the heavy use of egg yolk; second, wine; and third, candles.

1. Sabbath Foods

Challah bread is the one essential food for the Sabbath, and it is prepared in a braided form for most Sabbaths. Two loaves are used to symbolize the double portion of the manna that God gave for the Sabbath day. Every day, He gave one portion of manna, except on Friday, when He gave two portions to cover the needs for both Friday and Saturday.

As the Sabbath begins to draw nigh on Friday night, the *challah* bread is broken with a special blessing over it, and it is then dipped in salt before it is eaten, because all sacrifices were salted. The name *challah* itself means "round loaf" or "cake", and it represents the share or loaf given to the priest during the time when the Tabernacle stood and later the Temple. Subsequently, the Sabbath loaf retained its old Hebrew name, although it was no longer given to priests.

Among traditional Sabbath food is fish. Any kind of *kosher* meat is permitted, but according to the rabbis, fish is to be preferred for several reasons: God promised that Israel will multiply "like the sand of the sea", and fish comes from the sea. The word "fish" has the numerical value of seven in Hebrew, which equals the seventh day of the week. And lastly, just as God always watches over Israel, the eye of the fish is always open.

Another type of food for the Sabbath is known as *kugel*, which is a pudding or a casserole of rice or noodles mixed with raisins.

Another specialty food is known as *cholent*, which comes from a word that means "warm." This is food that is kept warm from Friday into the Sabbath, so the families can enjoy a warm meal for the Sabbath day.

2. Sabbath Lights

The second essential element for the Sabbath observance in Judaism is lights. Why lights? Originally, the lighting of lamps was a Jewish protest against the Babylonian Sabbath, for which neither fire nor lights were used. In ancient times, the last act before the Sabbath began was the kindling of the lights, because it was prohibited to kindle fire on the Sabbath. Originally, the intent was only to provide light for that day, but eventually, it was associated with the Sabbath. Later, the rabbis reinterpreted it as symbolizing the weekly refilling and rekindling of the lampstand in the Temple. Today, candles are lit to symbolize the joy that fills the Jewish home on this day. The creation of light was the first work of God, and God rested from His work of creation on the Sabbath day. Furthermore, according to Judaism, when Adam and Eve sinned, the great light of creation was extinguished. The Sabbath lights manifest the Jewish longing to return to a state of sinlessness, when the first light will reappear in the world to come.

What about the number of lights? In most Jewish homes today, two candles are lit. Historically, the reason was that in the average Jewish home in *Talmudic* times, there were just three rooms: the kitchen, the living room, and the bedroom. Before the Sabbath began, one light was lit in the kitchen and one light in the living room. In the bedroom, no candle was lit, for once the Sabbath began, one could not extinguish the light. Obviously, one did not want to have a lighted candle while sleeping. Eventually, lighting the two candles, one for the kitchen and one for the living room, became an established religious rite. Later it was reinterpreted by the rabbis to represent the two versions of the Sabbath commandment: first, Exodus 20:8, which states: *Remember the sabbath day*; and second, Deuteronomy 5:12, which states: *Observe the sabbath day*. The norm today is two candles; some Jewish homes light seven, while others light ten.

The one who kindles the Sabbath lights is generally the woman. It is uniquely the responsibility of the woman to light the candles. According to the rabbis, when Adam fell, it was really the woman who caused the light to be extinguished, so it is now the woman who is responsible to bring the light back. After kindling the lights, and while saying the blessing, a woman covers her eyes with the palms of her hands. The reason for this is that normally all blessings are recited before the rite or the act itself in Judaism. However, on the Sabbath the woman first kindles the fire and then recites the blessing, because once the Sabbath has been ushered in with the blessing, the kindling of lights is forbidden since that would be work. Because the blessing must precede the act, she shields her eyes with the palms of her hands so as not to see or to benefit from the light until after the blessing. This also, according to Judaism, will aid in devotion during prayer.

As she lights the candles and covers her eyes, she will say the following blessing:

> *Blessed are You, O Lord our God, King of the universe, Who has sanctified us with Your commandments and commanded us to kindle the lights of the Holy Sabbath.*

3. Sabbath Wine

Wine is the third essential element required for the Sabbath observance; everyone will drink a certain small portion of wine. This will be preceded by the recitation of a blessing:

> *Blessed are You, O Lord our God, King of the universe, Who created the fruit of the vine.*

The expression "fruit of the vine" in Judaism does not refer to grape juice. It refers to real wine that comes from the fruit of the grape. Judaism uses the expression "fruit of the vine" on special occasions.

E. The Meals of the Sabbath

The Sabbath is an occasion for eating. Altogether one will eat three meals on the Sabbath day. There is also a tradition of eating a fourth meal before the Sabbath actually comes to an end. The first meal is eaten on Friday night, the second meal is eaten on Saturday morning, and the third meal is eaten on Saturday afternoon following the synagogue service.

The Sabbath tablecloth is always white. The history of this custom has to do with the fact that tablecloths were used only on festive occasions in ancient times, and these were usually white. Eventually, the Sabbath became associated with white tablecloths, and later this was reinterpreted to symbolize the manna, the color of which was white.

III. THE SABBATH IN GENESIS

A major argument used to support mandatory Sabbath observance is based on the concept that the Sabbath is a creation ordinance. The passage used is Genesis 2:2-3.

> ²*And on the seventh day God finished his work which he had made; and he rested on the seventh day from all his work which he had made.* ³*And God blessed the seventh day, and hallowed it; because that in it he rested from all his work which God had created and made.*

A. The Exposition

Several things should be noted concerning the exposition of the key passage: With the end of the sixth day, God finished His creative work. He then rested on the seventh day, not in the sense that He was tired, but in the sense of "ceasing." As noted before, the Hebrew word *shabbat* means not only "to rest," it also means "to cease." God "sabbathed," meaning He rested in the sense of ceasing from His creative work. God did two things to the seventh day: He blessed it, and He *hallowed* or sanctified it. The reason He blessed it is because God rested on that day; He ceased from all His creative work. This is the only reference to the Sabbath in the whole Book of Genesis, and it is not called a "Sabbath" but only *the seventh day*. The verbal form of the term used means "cessation", but the noun is not used in this text. There is no command to observe the Sabbath in Genesis. And lastly, the emphasis is on rest and cessation, not on observance.

B. The Issue

The issue is this: Is the Sabbath a creation ordinance? At this point, let us assume that the Sabbath is a creation ordinance. If so, it would mean that it is obligatory for both Jews and Gentiles, since it was given before there was any distinction between Jews and Gentiles—a distinction that only began with Genesis 12, not Genesis 2.

Furthermore, even if it were a creation ordinance, it would not mean it is obligatory upon all. For example, one thing that certainly is a creation ordinance is marriage (Gen. 2:23-25). However, it is not mandatory for every individual because celibacy or singleness is a coequal, even a superior, option (Mat. 19:10-12; I Cor. 7:1-7). If the Sabbath were a creation ordinance, then these things would also be true.

However, the truth is that the Sabbath is not a creation ordinance and this can be seen in six ways. First, the crucial term *shabbat* or "Sabbath" is not even mentioned. At this point, there is no use of the word *shabbat*; the day is only referred to as *the seventh day*.

The second way this is seen is that there is no mention of man's being involved in the rest. There is only a mention of God's resting.

The third way this is seen is that the seventh day does mark a climax. However, the climax is not the creation of man, but it is God's own triumphal rest. God's own triumphal rest is what makes this day unique.

The fourth way this is seen is that there is no command in the Book of Genesis to observe the seventh day; it only states what God did on the seventh day. It is not found among the Noahic commandments or among the commands God gave to Abraham, Isaac, or Jacob. Furthermore, there is no record of its practice between Adam and Moses.

The fifth way this is seen is that the Sabbath is never treated as a creation ordinance in the New Testament. Mark 2:27 states:

The sabbath was made for man, and not man for the sabbath.

Some try to use this verse to prove that the Sabbath was a creation ordinance. However, the point of this verse is not to deal with the origin of the Sabbath, but to deal with the purpose of the Sabbath: *The sabbath was made for man*. Furthermore, what *Yeshua* said was to contradict the pharisaic teaching that Israel was created for the purpose of honoring the Sabbath. A second passage used to try to prove that the Sabbath was a creation ordinance is Hebrews 4:3-4, but this passage is simply teaching about salvation rest on the basis of the Old Testament. The Book of Hebrews treats Genesis eschatologically for salvation rest, not as a creation ordinance. It also treats the Genesis Sabbath typologically as the future Kingdom or heavenly rest.

And sixth, yes, God did bless and sanctify the Sabbath, but the blessing and sanctification of the seventh day was to emphasize rest and cessation of work, not as an observance.

Commenting on this point, Lewis Sperry Chafer wrote:

> It is incredible that this great institution of the Sabbath could have existed during all those centuries and there be no mention of it in the scriptures dealing with that time. The words of Job, who lived 500 years and more before Moses, offer an illustration. His experience discloses the spiritual life of the pre-Mosaic saint, having no written scriptures, and striving to know his whole duty to God. Job and his friends refer to creation, the flood, and many details of human obligation to God; but not once do they mention the Sabbath. Again, it is impossible that this great institution, with all that it contemplated of relationship between God and man, could have existed at that time and not have been mentioned at any portion of the argument of the book of Job.[2]

Writing along similar lines, Dr. Charles L. Feinberg states:

> There are some who find a reference to the institution of the Sabbath at creation. . . It will be noted that there is no hint that God gave the Sabbath to man. He alone rested. . . Not only do those who keep the seventh day try to read into this passage the institution of the original Sabbath for all mankind, but even others go to this passage for their supposed authority for the Lord's Day. They reason that if the Sabbath received its authority here, and the observance of the seventh day has been changed to the first day, then the observance of the first day must go back to Genesis 2 for its authority. Another fact that militates against the view that the Sabbath began in Eden is that we find no mention of it for centuries later. . .

---

[2] Lewis Sperry Chafer, *Grace: An Exposition of God's Marvelous Love* (Nabu Press, 2010), 186.

A study of the period between Adam and Moses, a period of about 2,500 years, will reveal that the institution of the Sabbath is not mentioned anywhere. . . . If the Sabbath did exist, then it is more than passing strange that, although we find accounts of religious life and the worship of the patriarchs, in which accounts mention is specifically made to the rite of circumcision, the sacrifices, the offering of the tithe, and the institution of marriage, we should find no mention of the great institution of the Sabbath. It did not exist. . .[3]

In the New Testament, Genesis 2:2-3 is not treated as a creation ordinance, but it is treated eschatologically of Messiah's salvation rest. Hebrews 4:3-4 uses the passage to teach that salvation rest is rooted in the Old Testament.

It also interprets typologically the future, heavenly rest, as Harold H. P. Dressler states:

Genesis 2 does not teach a "creation ordinance" . . . the institution of the Sabbath for the people of Israel, however, was based on the creation account and became a sign of God's redemptive goal for mankind.[4]

Finally, several observations can be made on the issue of the Sabbath being a creation ordinance. The Sabbath rest law is not found in the Edenic Covenant, the covenant God made with Adam in Eden. It is also not found in the Adamic Covenant, the covenant God made with Adam after his expulsion from the Garden. Furthermore, it is not found in the Noahic Covenant, the covenant God made with Noah after the Flood. The Abrahamic Covenant too does not contain a Sabbath law. God made this covenant with Abraham, with whom the Jewish people began. There is also no record of anyone observing the Sabbath throughout the Book of Genesis, from Adam to Moses. Lastly, there is the example of Job, a

---

[3] Charles Lee Feinberg, "The Sabbath and the Lord's Day," *Bibliotheca Sacra* Apr. (1938): 172-194 (here 180-181).
[4] Harold H. P. Dressler, "The Sabbath in the Old Testament," in *From Sabbath to Lord's Day: A Biblical, Historical and Theological Investigation* (ed. D. A. Carson; Grand Rapids: Zondervan, 1982), 30.

pre-Mosaic saint. There is no mention of the Sabbath, although Job does mention things in the Book of Genesis such as the Creation, the Flood, and many details concerning man's obligation to God.

So, concerning the issue: Is the Sabbath a creation ordinance? One can draw three conclusions: First, the Sabbath is not a creation ordinance; second, the institution of the Sabbath for the people of Israel was based on the creation account; and third, it thus became an eschatological sign of salvation rest and God's redemptive goal for mankind.

C. Summary

To summarize how the Book of Genesis introduces the Sabbath, several points can be noted. There is no use of the term *shabbat* or "Sabbath" in the Book of Genesis; it uses only the term *the seventh day*. There is no command that it be observed as a day of rest. There is no record of anyone's keeping the seventh day prior to Moses. The seventh day is emphasized as a day of rest and cessation from work, but not as a day of observance. There is no basis for mandatory Sabbath observance for Jews or Gentiles on the basis of Genesis 2. If the Sabbath were a creation ordinance, it would be obligatory for Jews and Gentiles, not just Jewish believers.

IV. THE SABBATH IN THE LAW OF MOSES

The Hebrew Old Testament is divided into three sections: the Law of Moses, the Prophets, and the Writings. This chapter will focus on the Law of Moses.

A. The Passages

1. Exodus 16:23-30

[23]And he said unto them, This is that which Jehovah has spoken, Tomorrow is a solemn rest, a holy sabbath unto Jehovah: bake that which ye will bake, and boil that which ye will boil; and all that remains over lay up for you to be kept until the morning. [24]And they laid it up till the morning, as Moses bade: and it did not become foul, neither was there any worm therein. [25]And Moses said, Eat that to-day; for to-day is a sabbath unto Jehovah: to-day ye shall not find it in the field. [26]Six days ye shall gather it; but on the seventh day is the sabbath, in it there shall be none. [27]And it came to pass on the seventh day, that there went out some of the people to gather, and they found none. [28]And Jehovah said unto Moses, How long refuse ye to keep my commandments and my laws? [29]See, for that Jehovah has given you the sabbath, therefore he gives you on the sixth day the bread of two days; abide ye every man in his place, let no man go out of his place on the seventh day. [30]So the people rested on the seventh day.

This passage deals primarily with the prohibition of gathering manna on the Sabbath day. In verse 23, God told Moses that the following day was *a solemn rest, a holy sabbath*, so they were to prepare for it on the sixth day. Verse 24 promised that the manna gathered on the sixth day for the Sabbath would not spoil. Verse 25 states that there would be no manna in the field on the Sabbath. Therefore, in verse 26, they were to gather manna for six days, but on the seventh day there would be no manna. According to verse 27, some did go out to gather on the seventh day, but found none. In verse 28, this was disobedience. In verse 29, God had now given them the Sabbath; therefore, God will give a double portion of manna on the sixth day. On the seventh day, everyone should abide in his own home. In verse 30, therefore, the people rested on the seventh day.

What does all this teach? The Sabbath observance, as an observance, began only with Moses. This passage of Exodus 16 contains the first occurrence of both the word *shabbat* and the concept of the Sabbath as a day of rest, for the word was not used in the Book of Genesis. Only now is there a concept of rest on the Sabbath for man. It is here in the Hebrew text that the full form is found for the first time: *shabbaton shabbat kodesh*, meaning "a solemn rest, a holy sabbath," "a sabbatical celebration." The reason the full form is given is that it was not known before this time. In the Hebrew text, there is no definite article; grammatically, this implies that it was not known before this time. The text literally states, "tomorrow is a rest of a holy sabbath." The specific command was not to gather manna on the Sabbath. The fact that so many disobeyed this rule implies that the people were not used to resting on the Sabbath day.

2. Exodus 20:8-11

[8] *Remember the sabbath day, to keep it holy.* [9] *Six days shall you labor, and do all your work;* [10] *but the seventh day is a sabbath unto Jehovah your God: in it you shall not do any work, you, nor your son, nor your daughter, your man-servant, nor your maid-servant, nor your cattle, nor your stranger that is within your gates:* [11] *for in six days Jehovah made heaven and earth, the sea, and all that in them is, and rested the seventh day: wherefore Jehovah blessed the sabbath day, and hallowed it.*

This passage contains the fourth commandment, and six observations can be made. The first observation is that God used the word *Remember* in verse 8, not as a reference back to Genesis 2, but as a reference to its nearest context, Exodus 16. He can now say *Remember*, since it was already mentioned in chapter 16. However, in

Deuteronomy 5:12, which does not have the same context, He used the word *Observe*, rather than *Remember*.

The second observation, also in verse 8, is that they were *to keep it holy*; they were to keep it as a special day, separated from all others as a day dedicated to God.

The third observation (verses 9-10) is that the key way to keep it holy was cessation from work. This included family members, servants, strangers, and domesticated animals. God rested on the seventh day, and so Israel and what belongs to Israel is to rest on the seventh day.

The fourth observation (verse 11) is that only now is the word *shabbat* applied to *the seventh day* of Genesis 2:2-3. Again, this does not mean that the Sabbath of the seventh day of Genesis 2 had already been set aside for humanity. The word *wherefore* in Hebrew is *al kein*, which means that the present command was based upon a previous event. The previous event was the fact that God rested on the seventh day, but it does not mean the command itself was previously in force at the time of the event. The construction causally connects an event of the past with a situation or command in the present.

The fifth observation is that there is no obligation here to corporately worship God on this day; the Sabbath was not a day of corporate worship, but a day of rest.

And the sixth observation is that this was not a day of total inactivity, but a day of rest and refreshment. The rest itself was an act of worship; corporate worship was not a factor in the Old Testament Sabbath.

3. Exodus 23:12

Six days you shall do your work, and on the seventh day you shall rest; [the purpose was] *that your ox and your ass may have rest, and the son of your handmaid, and the sojourner, may be refreshed.*

This verse contains a short summary concerning the Sabbath law, and three observations can be made: First, the emphasis of this passage is again on rest and refreshment; second, it includes both man and animal; and third, there is no command for corporate worship.

4. Exodus 31:12-17

This passage provides some details concerning the Sabbath law. In verse 12, God spoke to Moses. In verse 13, He told him to speak to the children of Israel that they keep His Sabbaths. The reason was that it was a sign between God and Israel throughout their generations that they may know that Jehovah is the One who sanctifies them. Then in verses 14-17, God adds:

> *14 Ye shall keep the sabbath therefore; for it is holy unto you: every one that profanes it shall surely be put to death; for whosoever does any work therein, that soul shall be cut off from among his people. 15 Six days shall work be done; but on the seventh day is a sabbath of solemn rest, holy to Jehovah: whosoever does any work on the sabbath day, he shall surely be put to death. 16 Wherefore the children of Israel shall keep the sabbath, to observe the sabbath throughout their generations, for a perpetual covenant. 17 It is a sign between me and the children of Israel for ever: for in six days Jehovah made heaven and earth, and on the seventh day he rested, and was refreshed.*

There are seven observations concerning these verses. First, this passage follows the instructions concerning the Tabernacle. The work on the Tabernacle was holy work, but the law of the Sabbath still applies and supersedes it, so they could not even do this holy work on the Sabbath day. Second, the Sabbath is now called an *ot*, meaning a "sign" between God and Israel. The Sabbath is a sign that it is God who sanctifies or sets Israel apart from all other nations. It is a sign that God ceased to work after six days and rested on the seventh. As a sign, it could only be meant for Israel. It is a memorial of Creation. It is a sign of God's covenant-relationship to Israel. Third, the Sabbath is a *perpetual covenant*, for it is a sign of the Mosaic Covenant. It is *perpetual*, meaning it was to be in existence as long as the Mosaic Covenant was in effect. Fourth, the penalty for disobedience was *death*. Fifth, the specific command was cessation from work. Sixth, profaning the Sabbath meant to work on the Sabbath and thus consider the Sabbath like any other day.

They were to do no work, but to stay at home. And seventh, there is no command for corporate worship.

5. Exodus 34:21

Six days you shall work, but on the seventh day you shall rest: in plowing time and in harvest you shall rest.

This passage prohibits plowing or reaping on the Sabbath day, and four observations can be made. First, the Sabbath law applied even during the critical times of plowing and harvest. Second, this is a short summary that came with the second set of tablets. Third, the main emphasis is that on the Sabbath day there must be a cessation of all farm work. And fourth, there is no command for corporate worship.

6. Exodus 35:1-3

The main point of this passage is that there was to be no kindling of fire on the Sabbath day. According to verse 1, it is a command, and God states in verses 2-3:

²Six days shall work be done; but on the seventh day there shall be to you a holy day, a sabbath of solemn rest to Jehovah: whosoever does any work therein shall be put to death. ³Ye shall kindle no fire throughout your habitations upon the sabbath day.

Several observations are made in this passage: The Sabbath day is mandatory. It is *a holy day*. Furthermore, the Sabbath is a day of *solemn rest*. Violating it incurs the death penalty. The command proper is that there be no kindling of fire on the Sabbath day. Finally, there is no command for corporate worship on this day.

7. Leviticus 16:31

It is a sabbath of solemn rest unto you, and ye shall afflict your souls; it is a statute for ever.

This passage deals with the Sabbath of the Day of Atonement. It teaches that the Day of Atonement is to be treated as *a sabbath*. This is the only time that the term *sabbath* is used of a day that is not the seventh day of the week.

8. Leviticus 19:3

Ye shall fear every man his mother, and his father; and ye shall keep my sabbaths: I am Jehovah your God.

This passage has a basic command: *Ye shall keep my sabbaths.* By using the word *my* in this passage, God is claiming the Sabbath day as His own.

9. Leviticus 19:30

Ye shall keep my sabbaths, and reverence my sanctuary: I am Jehovah.

This passage emphasizes the basic command: *Ye shall keep my sabbaths.* God again claimed the day for Himself.

10. Leviticus 23:3

Six days shall work be done: but on the seventh day is a sabbath of solemn rest, a holy convocation; ye shall do no manner of work: it is a sabbath unto Jehovah in all your dwellings.

This passage correlates the Sabbath with the feasts of Israel, and five observations can be made. First, there are two names for this day, *a sabbath of solemn rest* and *a holy convocation.* Second, this passage comes just before the discussion on the seven Holy Seasons of Israel, showing that the Sabbath laws must apply even if a holy day falls on the Sabbath day. Third, the command proper is that it is a day of rest, when no work was allowed. Fourth, there is no command here for corporate worship, only a day of rest *in all your dwellings.* And fifth, it is *a holy convocation.* Whatever *convocation* may mean, it is clearly stated that it is to be observed *in all your dwellings*, meaning their homes.

The expression *holy convocation* is sometimes used to teach corporate worship on the Sabbath day. However, this term does not mean "corporate worship," for it is used of the Passover in Leviticus 23:4, as well as other festivals, which had to do with family gatherings, not corporate worship. In most cases it is a reference to the gathering of the priesthood for the special sacrifices to be offered on this occasion, a fact we will discuss further later in this chapter.

11. Leviticus 23:11

... and he shall wave the sheaf before Jehovah, to be accepted for you: on the morrow after the sabbath the priest shall wave it.

This passage deals with the Sabbath in conjunction with the Feast of Firstfruits. This feast was to be observed *on the morrow after the sabbath*, meaning on the first day of the week. The point is that the Feast of Firstfruits was to be observed on the first day of the week—our Sunday today—following the Sabbath which, in turn, followed Passover. Simply put, this feast was to be observed on the first Sunday after Passover.

12. Leviticus 23:15-16

[15]And ye shall count unto you from the morrow after the sabbath, from the day that ye brought the sheaf of the wave-offering; seven sabbaths shall there be complete: [16]even unto the morrow after the seventh sabbath shall ye number fifty days [from the Feast of Firstfruits to the Feast of Weeks]; *and ye shall offer a new meal-offering unto Jehovah.*

This passage deals with the Sabbath in conjunction with the Feast of Weeks or Pentecost. The Feast of Weeks is to be observed seven weeks, plus one day, following the Feast of Firstfruits. Pentecost was counted by the number of Sabbaths.

13. Leviticus 23:32

It shall be unto you a sabbath of solemn rest, and ye shall afflict your souls: in the ninth day of the month at even, from even unto even, shall ye keep your sabbath.

This passage deals with the Sabbath of the Day of Atonement. This is not a reference to a weekly Sabbath, but shows again that the only time the term *shabbat* was applied to a day other than the seventh day of the week was the Day of Atonement.

14. Leviticus 23:38

. . . besides the sabbaths of Jehovah, besides your gifts, and besides all your vows, and besides all your freewill-offerings, which ye give unto Jehovah.

This passage makes a passing reference to *the sabbaths of Jehovah*, meaning they are His Sabbaths. The point is that the offerings for the seven Holy Seasons of Israel are in addition to the Sabbath offerings, not in place of them.

15. Leviticus 24:5-9

This passage connects the Sabbath with the shewbread, especially verse 8:

Every sabbath day he shall set it in order before Jehovah continually; it is on the behalf of the children of Israel, an everlasting covenant.

Two observations can be made from this verse. First, that on every Sabbath, the priest had to lay out the shewbread. And second, that this was a ceremonial facet of the Sabbath commandment.

16. Leviticus 26:2

This passage is exactly the same as those in chapter 19:3 and 30:

Ye shall keep my sabbaths, and reverence my sanctuary: I am Jehovah.

17. Numbers 15:32-36

[32] And while the children of Israel were in the wilderness, they found a man gathering sticks upon the sabbath day. [33] And they that found him gathering sticks brought him unto Moses and Aaron, and unto all the congregation. [34] And they put him in ward, because it had not been declared what should be done to him. [35] And Jehovah said unto Moses, The man shall surely

be put to death: all the congregation shall stone him with stones without the camp. ³⁶And all the congregation brought him without the camp, and stoned him to death with stones; as Jehovah commanded Moses.

This passage deals with an execution for violating the Sabbath law. In verse 32, a man was found *gathering sticks upon the sabbath day*. In verse 33, the violator was brought before Moses and Aaron and the whole congregation of Israel. In verse 34, he was placed under arrest. At the inquiry of Moses, God answered in verse 35, and in verse 36 the man was executed.

Two observations can be made: First, this re-emphasizes the death penalty for violating the Sabbath law; and second, the specific command that was violated was the picking up of sticks on the Sabbath day.

18. Numbers 28:9-10

⁹And on the sabbath day [they were to offer] two he-lambs a year old without blemish, and two tenth parts of an ephah of fine flour for a meal-offering, mingled with oil, and the drink-offering thereof: ¹⁰this is the burnt-offering of every sabbath, besides the continual burnt-offering, and the drink-offering thereof.

This passage deals with Sabbath offerings. It emphasizes the ceremonial facet of the Mosaic Law. It also shows that, for the priests, the Sabbath was not a day of rest, but a day of work.

19. Deuteronomy 5:12-15

¹²Observe the sabbath day, to keep it holy, as Jehovah your God commanded you. ¹³Six days shall you labor, and do all your work; ¹⁴but the seventh day is a sabbath unto Jehovah your God: in it you shall not do any work, you, nor your son, nor your daughter, nor your man-servant, nor your maid-servant, nor your ox, nor your ass, nor any of your cattle, nor your stranger that is within your gates; that your man-servant and your maid-servant may rest as well as you. ¹⁵And you shall remember that you were a servant in the land of Egypt, and Jehovah your God brought you out thence by a mighty hand and by an outstretched arm: therefore Jehovah your God commanded you to keep the sabbath day.

This passage is a reiteration of the fourth commandment, given in the Book of Exodus. Verses 12 and 13 give the command, and in verse 14, no one is allowed to do any work on the Sabbath day. In verse 15, they are to remember that they were servants in the land of Egypt, and that Jehovah, the God of Israel, brought them out of Egypt *by a mighty hand and by an outstretched arm.* For that reason, *Jehovah your God commanded you to keep the sabbath day.*

From this passage, there are six things to be noted. First, the key distinction between the fourth commandment in Deuteronomy as over against the fourth commandment in the Book of Exodus is that here it states: *Observe the sabbath*, whereas in Exodus it states: *Remember the sabbath.* In Exodus 20, God said to *Remember* the Sabbath, because within the Book of Exodus, the Sabbath was already mentioned in chapter 16. However, within the framework of Deuteronomy, there was no previous mention of the Sabbath, so it is *Observe* the Sabbath day rather than *Remember* it. Furthermore, while the Book of Exodus lists various groups that cannot work, Deuteronomy adds that neither the ox nor the ass is allowed to work, an addition to the Exodus account.

The second thing to be noted is that this passage is a reminder of the Exodus commandment.

The third thing is that the commandment proper is a cessation of labor. That includes family members, servants, strangers—Gentiles living in the Land—and all domesticated animals.

Fourth, the background to this command includes several things: Israel was once a servant to Egypt with no day of rest. God delivered Israel and brought her out of the land of Egypt. Because of the Exodus experience, God commanded Israel to keep the Sabbath. For the same reason, the servants must also rest on this day.

The fifth thing to be noted about this passage is that the Sabbath is a sign of the Exodus; it is a sign that God brought Israel out of the land of Egypt. The Sabbath is to be kept as a sign and a memorial of the Exodus experience. For this reason, the Sabbath can only be related to Israel, since only Israel was delivered from the land of Egypt. God did not deliver the Church in general from Egypt, nor did He deliver the Seventh Day Adventists in particular from Egypt.

And the sixth thing to be noted is that, again, there is no command for corporate worship.

B. The Sabbath Commandment Proper

In the Law of Moses, there are seven aspects to the Sabbath commandment. The first aspect is positive; the Sabbath commandment specified a day of rest. The second aspect is negative; the Sabbath commandment meant no labor whatsoever.

The third aspect is to note five specifics of what not to do on the Sabbath day: There was to be no gathering of manna (Ex. 16:23-30); there was to be no traveling (Ex. 16:29); there was to be no plowing or reaping (Ex. 34:21); there was to be no kindling of fire (Ex. 35:3); and there was to be no gathering of wood (Num. 15:32).

The fourth aspect about the Sabbath commandment is that there was a major exception to the "no labor rule" in that the Sabbath was not a day of rest for the priesthood. They had to work more on this day than on the regular days.

The fifth aspect is that there was a penalty for profaning the Sabbath: death. To profane the Sabbath was to treat it like any day.

The sixth aspect is that the one thing missing from every Sabbath passage is a command for corporate worship. There was not a single command for corporate worship anywhere in these passages.

The seventh aspect is that the wrongful applications of the Sabbath commandment can be seen in two ways: first, in the inconsistencies of Sabbath-keeping, and second, in the misapplication of corporate worship.

1. The Inconsistencies

If a person insists on keeping the Sabbath on the basis of the Law of Moses, then consistency demands that he keep all the facets that the

Mosaic Law required concerning the Sabbath. But what most Sabbath-keepers tend to do on the Sabbath is precisely what the Law of Moses forbade; for example, they do not stay home, but travel to corporate worship.

They do insist on keeping the Sabbath as a day of corporate worship, which is exactly what the Law of Moses did not require. It is also inconsistent to base Sabbath-keeping on the Law of Moses and then fail to keep it in the manner prescribed by the Law of Moses. Sabbath-keepers are forced to make so many adjustments concerning the Sabbath law that, in the end, these adjustments actually violate the Law of Moses rather than keep it; for instance, they travel to a church or congregational meeting on the Sabbath day.

The Sabbath was not a day of corporate worship. While the rest required on that day might itself have been an act of worship, corporate worship was not a factor for the Sabbath in the Law of Moses. Nor can Sabbath-keepers claim that the use of the term *holy convocation* teaches corporate worship, since it had to do with a family gathering and priestly rituals, not acts of corporate worship. The Law mandated corporate worship only on three occasions: the Feast of Passover, the Feast of Weeks or Pentecost, and the Feast of Tabernacles. Even on these occasions, the "corporate" facet was family, not whole congregations. While these feasts were to be observed at Jerusalem, they were observed as family units. Corporate worship was to be at the Tabernacle or Temple, wherever it stood. Initially, it was at Shiloh, but later, it took place in Jerusalem. Hence, corporate worship on a weekly Sabbath was physically impossible under the Law.

The last inconsistency is that if the Sabbath commandment were mandatory on the basis of the Law, then it is only mandatory as a day of rest, not as a day to hold congregational meetings of corporate worship.

2. The Misapplications

The second way the wrongful application of the Sabbath commandment manifests itself is in its misapplication to corporate worship. In the Law of Moses, the Sabbath was a day of rest and cessation from labors, not a day of corporate worship. Nevertheless, that is the area where some claim the Sabbath law still applies. But that was simply not the purpose of the Sabbath commandment in the Law of Moses. The Sabbath synagogue services as found in the New Testament originated with the Babylonian Captivity, not with the Law of Moses. Under the Law, the Sabbath was a day of rest and refreshment from the regular work of the other six days. While the rest itself may have been an act of worship, corporate worship on the Sabbath was not a factor in the Old Testament.

The one passage used to try to substantiate corporate worship on the Sabbath is Leviticus 23:3, which refers to the Sabbath as a *holy convocation*. The phrase *a holy convocation* is often found in connection with the Sabbath and, as noted before, is sometimes used as the basis for teaching that the Sabbath was a day of corporate worship for all. However, this phrase was used only in conjunction with the priesthood and sacrifices. The corporate connotation pertained mostly to the priests; the place of this corporate worship was in the Tabernacle or Temple, and it was for the purpose of sacrifices. Since only the priesthood could do the work of sacrificing, the *holy convocation* applied only to them.

The phrase is found a total of nineteen times, all in three books of Moses: Exodus, Leviticus, and Numbers. Two are found in Exodus; eleven of the nineteen in chapter 23 of the Book of Leviticus; and six others are found in chapters 28 and 29 of the Book of Numbers.

The first and second times the phrase is found are in Exodus 12:16:

And in the first day there shall be to you a holy convocation, and in the seventh day a holy convocation; no manner of work shall be done in them, save that which every man must eat, that only may be done by you.

The first and seventh days of the Feast of Unleavened Bread were to be *a holy convocation*. This involved abstaining from work. While no sacrifices are mentioned here, they will be mentioned for this occasion later.

The third time the phrase is used is in Leviticus 23:2:

Speak unto the children of Israel, and say unto them, The set feasts of Jehovah, which ye shall proclaim to be holy convocations, even these are my set feasts.

This verse declares that the *set feasts* or "Holy Seasons" are to be *holy convocations*. As the chapter shows, they are all connected with sacrifices.

The fourth usage of the phrase is in Leviticus 23:3:

> *Six days shall work be done: but on the seventh day is a sabbath of solemn rest, a holy convocation; ye shall do no manner of work: it is a sabbath unto Jehovah in all your dwellings.*

This is a reference to the Sabbath as a *holy convocation*; it was a day of doubling the daily sacrifices and a day of rest.

The fifth usage of the phrase is a restatement of verse 2 that the *set feasts* or Holy Seasons are *holy convocations* in Leviticus 23:4:

> *These are the set feasts of Jehovah, even holy convocations, which ye shall proclaim in their appointed season.*

The sixth and seventh times the phrase is mentioned are in Leviticus 23:7-8:

> *[7]In the first day ye shall have a holy convocation: ye shall do no servile work. [8]But ye shall offer an offering made by fire unto Jehovah seven days: in the seventh day is a holy convocation; ye shall do no servile work.*

Again, this is a reference to the first and seventh days of the Feast of Unleavened Bread as in the Exodus passage. On both days, work is prohibited. It was a time to *offer an offering made by fire unto Jehovah seven days*, and it took a convocation of priests to offer these sacrifices.

The eighth reference to the phrase is in Leviticus 23:21:

> *And ye shall make proclamation on the selfsame day; there shall be a holy convocation unto you; ye shall do no servile work: it is a statute for ever in all your dwellings throughout your generations.*

This *holy convocation* is a reference to the Feast of Weeks or Pentecost and here, too, it was to be a day of rest. The previous verses, 17-20, show this to be a day of sacrifices for which the priesthood would have to convene.

The ninth reference to the phrase is in Leviticus 23:24:

Speak unto the children of Israel, saying, In the seventh month, on the first day of the month, shall be a solemn rest unto you, a memorial of blowing of trumpets, a holy convocation.

This reference is to the Feast of Trumpets, which is a *holy convocation* when no work is permitted, and in verse 25, the priesthood had to *offer an offering made by fire unto Jehovah*.

The tenth reference to the phrase is in Leviticus 23:27:

Howbeit on the tenth day of this seventh month is the day of atonement: it shall be a holy convocation unto you, and ye shall afflict your souls; and ye shall offer an offering made by fire unto Jehovah.

This is a reference to the Day of Atonement, which is a *holy convocation*, for no work was allowed; they were to *offer an offering made by fire unto Jehovah*.

The eleventh and twelfth references to the phrase are in Leviticus 23:35-36:

³⁵On the first day shall be a holy convocation: ye shall do no servile work. ³⁶Seven days ye shall offer an offering made by fire unto Jehovah: on the eighth day shall be a holy convocation unto you; and ye shall offer an offering made by fire unto Jehovah: it is a solemn assembly; ye shall do no servile work.

These *holy convocations* refer to the first and eighth days of the Feast of Tabernacles. Because no work was allowed on these days, they were considered holy convocations. Twice it is declared: *ye shall offer an offering made by fire unto Jehovah.*

The thirteenth reference to the phrase is in Leviticus 23:37:

> *These are the set feasts of Jehovah, which ye shall proclaim to be holy convocations, to offer an offering made by fire unto Jehovah, a burnt-offering, and a meal-offering, a sacrifice, and drink-offerings, each on its own day; . . .*

This is a restatement of verses 2 and 4 that the *set feasts* are *holy convocations.* It is clearly stated that the purpose of these *holy convocations* is to present offerings, a priestly function.

The remaining six passages are in chapters 28-29 of the Book of Numbers. They deal with the special sacrifices to be offered on the occasions of the *set feasts* or Holy Seasons of Leviticus 23.

The fourteen and fifteenth references to the phrase are in Numbers 28:18 and 25:

> *[18] In the first day shall be a holy convocation: ye shall do no servile work; . . .*
>
> ***
>
> *[25] And on the seventh day ye shall have a holy convocation: ye shall do no servile work.*

This is another reference to the first and seventh days of the Feast of Unleavened Bread; verses 19-24 detail the sacrifices and offerings for this occasion.

The sixteenth reference to the phrase is in Numbers 28:26:

> *Also in the day of the first-fruits, when ye offer a new meal-offering unto Jehovah in your feast of weeks, ye shall have a holy convocation; ye shall do no servile work; . . .*

This is a reference to the Feast of Firstfruits, and the following verses, 27-31, detail the sacrifices and offerings for the occasion.

The seventeenth reference to the phrase is in Numbers 29:1:

And in the seventh month, on the first day of the month, ye shall have a holy convocation; ye shall do no servile work: it is a day of blowing of trumpets unto you.

This reference is to the Feast of Trumpets; it is a *holy convocation*. The following verses, 2-6, spell out the sacrifices and offerings for this feast.

The eighteenth reference to the phrase is in Numbers 29:7:

And on the tenth day of this seventh month ye shall have a holy convocation; and ye shall afflict your souls: ye shall do no manner of work; . . .

This is a reference to the Day of Atonement; the special offerings for this occasion are then detailed in verses 8-11.

And the nineteenth reference to the phrase is Numbers 29:12:

And on the fifteenth day of the seventh month ye shall have a holy convocation; ye shall do no servile work, and ye shall keep a feast unto Jehovah seven days: . . .

This final reference is to the Feast of Tabernacles; its special sacrifices are detailed in verses 13-38.

In all cases, the phrase *holy convocation* refers to a convocation of priests for the purpose of performing special sacrifices, and the Sabbath was one of those occasions. It was not a time of corporate worship for all Israel. The one passage used to try to substantiate corporate worship on the Sabbath is Leviticus 23:3, which refers to the Sabbath as a *holy convocation*. While it has relevance to family gatherings, these were not corporate acts of worship, as Dr. Louis Goldberg states:

On the Sabbath there was to be complete rest (physical) and holy convocation (spiritual refreshing) before the Lord.[5]

---

[5] Louis Goldberg, *Leviticus: Bible Study Commentary* (Grand Rapids: Zondervan, 1980), 116.

Concerning the Sabbath, even Leviticus 23:3 states: *it is a sabbath unto Jehovah in all your dwellings.* Again, the emphasis has to do with staying at home and resting as a family, rather than gathering together in corporate worship. As Dr. Goldberg also points out, the rest was also to include spiritual renewal. The expression *holy convocation* emphasized that on such occasions the priests were to offer special sacrifices.

In reality, the Mosaic Law mandated corporate worship only on three occasions: the feasts of Passover, Weeks, and Tabernacles, when they were to migrate to wherever the Tabernacle stood, either at Shiloh or later at Jerusalem where the Temple stood. Corporate worship by non-Levites was mandated only three times a year, not on a weekly Sabbath. This would have been physically impossible in light of the time it took to travel during biblical times. To profane the Sabbath was to consider it as any other day, and the penalty was death. Therefore, on the Sabbath they were to do no labor; they were to stay at home and rest (Ex. 16:29).

C. The Sabbath as a Sign

Four points underline that the Sabbath served as a sign. First, in the Law of Moses, the Sabbath was *a sign* or token of the Mosaic Covenant (Ex. 31:12-17). Covenants tended to have tokens or symbols related to them. For example, the rainbow was the token of the Noahic Covenant. Circumcision was the token of the Abrahamic Covenant. The Sabbath was a sign of God's sanctification of Israel, that Israel has been set apart from all other nations by the Mosaic Covenant. The Sabbath is a sign that God ceased working after six days, so the Jews are commanded to cease from work on the Sabbath day. The Sabbath in relation to Israel was a memorial of Creation, a sign of Israel's covenant relationship that began at Sinai.

The second point is that the Sabbath was a sign of the Exodus (Deut. 5:15), a sign and a memorial of the Exodus experience (Ezek. 20:10-12).

The third point is that no single event is given as the subject or the origin for the purpose of the Sabbath. Rather, a variety of things were given: a memorial of Creation, a memorial of the Exodus, a sign of Israel's sanctification, and a sign for the Mosaic Covenant.

And the fourth point is that since the Sabbath is a sign of the Mosaic Covenant, it is in force only for the duration of the covenant. If the covenant comes to an end, the sign is no longer obligatory.

To summarize all of the above: Because the Sabbath was a sign of the Mosaic Covenant—just as circumcision was a sign of the Abrahamic Covenant—it is obvious that the Sabbath can only be related to Israel, since only Israel was set apart at Sinai and only Israel has been delivered from the land of Egypt. God never delivered the Church in general out of Egypt or the Seventh Day Adventist Church in particular. In the context of the Mosaic Law, the Sabbath and the reasons for the Sabbath can only be related to the Jewish nation. The reasons given for Sabbath observance in the Law of Moses include: a memorial of Creation, a memorial of the Exodus, a sign of Israel's sanctification or setting apart as a nation, and a sign of the Mosaic Covenant. No one single event is given as the subject of its observance, but several. Because the Sabbath is a sign of the Mosaic Covenant, it is in force for the duration of the covenant. If there is a time when the covenant comes to an end, the sign would no longer be obligatory. This issue will be dealt with later.

D. The Ceremonial Aspects of the Sabbath

There were special ceremonial aspects to the observance of the Sabbath. Besides setting the day apart as a day of rest, it was to be a holy convocation within their dwellings. It was the day on which the new shewbread was put out (Lev. 24:8). Furthermore, it was a day of doubling the daily sacrifice (Num. 28:9-10). These ceremonial aspects of the Sabbath will become crucial when discussing the question of whether the Sabbath commandment is a moral or ceremonial issue.

E. The Features of the Sabbath

The Law of Moses deals with the nineteen features of the Sabbath. First, it was a day of physical rest, a day of cessation from the normal labors and activities.

The second feature is that the Sabbath in the Law of Moses was a sign of Israel as a separated people (Ex. 31:13).

Third, the Sabbath in the Law of Moses was a sign of the Mosaic Covenant (Ex. 31:12-17).

Fourth, the Sabbath in the Law of Moses itself is a covenant between God and Israel (Ex. 31:16).

Fifth, it is *perpetual* (Ex. 31:16). What exactly that means will be discussed in the next section.

Sixth, it is *for ever* (Ex. 31:17). Exactly what the Hebrew term *for ever* means will also be discussed in the next section.

Seventh, the Sabbath in the Law of Moses was a memorial of Creation for Israel (Ex. 20:11; 31:17).

Eight, the Sabbath in the Law of Moses is a sign of the Exodus (Deut. 5:15).

The ninth feature of the Sabbath in the Law of Moses is that the liberation of Israel from Egypt means that Israel is consecrated to God in a covenant-relationship, embodied in the Sabbath (Ex. 20:10; 31:15; 35:2; Lev. 19:3, 30; 23:3; 26:2; Deut. 5:15).

Tenth, the Sabbath in the Law of Moses might very well be the day of *gladness* of Numbers 10:10.

Eleventh, the Sabbath in the Law of Moses is a reminder of divine intervention. By means of divine intervention God broke into a world that was "waste and void," without form and empty. By divine intervention God began to fill the world, but rested on the seventh day. It is also a reminder that God, by divine intervention, brought about the Exodus experience.

Twelve, it also had social concerns; it included a day of rest for both man and animal. Even the slave in Israel was to be given that day off.

The thirteenth feature is that the Sabbath in the Law of Moses emphasizes God's authority so that violation of the Sabbath incurred the death penalty.

Fourteenth, the Sabbath observance began with Moses. There is no record in Scripture or outside of Scripture of anyone keeping a Sabbath prior to Moses. The Sabbath observance began with Moses.

Fifteenth, it was a holy day, a day set apart for God.

Sixteenth, it was a day of solemn rest. The concept of solemn rest was an emphasis on rest and refreshment. It was a day to rest and to be refreshed in preparation for another six-day workweek.

Seventeenth, God claimed the Sabbath as His own. On more than one occasion He said, "You will keep *My* Sabbaths." In this way, He claimed the Sabbath as His own special day.

Eighteenth, it was a day of special sacrifices and ceremonies. While there were sacrifices daily, all daily sacrifices were doubled on the Sabbath day. Furthermore, there was the ceremony of putting out the shewbread.

And the nineteenth feature of the Sabbath in the Law of Moses is that there was no command anywhere for corporate worship. It was not a day of corporate worship. It was a day for a holy convocation of families gathering within their dwellings. It was also a time for priests to come together and perform sacrifices.

F. The Perpetuity of the Sabbath

There are circles among both Jewish believers and Gentile believers who feel that the Sabbath is perpetual and therefore must be observed to this day. Some would insist that the Sabbath must be observed from sundown Friday to sundown Saturday, and others observe the Sabbath on Sunday, but both groups claim that the Sabbath is still mandatory.

1. The Basis

There are three key phrases found in conjunction with the Sabbath that are used as the basis for teaching that the Sabbath is perpetual. The first key phrase is *throughout your generations* (Ex. 31:13). The second key phrase is the term *perpetual* (Ex. 31:16), which is taken to mean "unending." The third key phrase is the term *for ever* (Ex. 31:17), which is taken to mean "eternal," and therefore still mandatory today.

The Hebrew word for the first key phrase *throughout your generations* is *ledorot*. While it is used of the Sabbath, this expression is also used of a man's lifetime (Lev. 25:30), of the Levitical Priesthood (Ex. 40:15; Lev. 6:22; 10:9; Num. 10:8; 18:23), of the ceremony of the lampstands (Ex. 27:21; Lev. 24:3), of the service of the brazen laver (Ex. 30:21), of the meal-offering (Lev. 6:18), and of the sacrificial system (Lev. 7:36; Num. 15:15).

The second key phrase used as a basis for teaching the perpetuity of the Sabbath is the term *perpetual*. The Hebrew word is either *tamid*, which means "perpetual", or *chok olam*, which means "a perpetual statute." This is not only used of the Sabbath, it is also used of the ceremony of the shewbread (Lev. 24:9), which everybody agrees has ended with Messiah's death.

The third key phrase is *for ever*. The simple, basic truth is that Classical Hebrew—the Hebrew of the Old Testament Scriptures—has no term that carries the concept of "eternity." There are phrases that carry this concept, such as "without end," but there is not a single word that carries the concept of eternity as there is in English.

To focus on the meaning of the term *for ever*, several things should be kept in mind. The Hebrew word is *olam*. The word itself simply means "long duration," "antiquity," "futurity," "until the end of a period of time." That period of time is determined by the context. Sometimes it is the length of a man's life, sometimes it is an age, sometimes it is a dispensation, and sometimes it refers to the end of human history.

There are two Hebrew forms of *olam*. The first form is *le-olam*, which means "unto an age." And the second form is *ad-olam*, which means "until an age." However, neither of these forms carries the English meaning of "forever." Although it has been translated that way in English, the Hebrew does not carry the concept of eternity as the English word "forever" does.

The word *olam*, *le-olam*, or *ad-olam*, sometimes means only up "to the end of a man's life." For example, it is used of someone's lifetime (Ex. 14:13), of a slave's life (Ex. 21:6; Lev. 25:46; Deut. 15:17), of Samuel's life (I Sam. 1:22; 2:35), of the lifetimes of David and Jonathan (I Sam. 20:23), and of David's lifetime (I Sam. 27:12; 28:2; I Chr. 28:4).

While the English reads *for ever*, obviously from the context it does not mean "forever" in the sense of eternity, but only up to the end of the person's life.

O*lam* sometimes means only "an age" or "dispensation." For example, Deuteronomy 23:3 uses the term *for ever* but limits the term to only ten generations. Here it obviously carries the concept of an age. In II Chronicles 7:16, it is used only for the period of the First Temple. So, again, the word *for ever* in Hebrew does not mean "eternal" as it does in English; it means up to the end of a period of time, either a man's life or an age or a dispensation.

The same word for "forever" is used of certain ceremonial facets of the Mosaic Law that everyone agrees have ended with the First Coming of the Messiah. For example, the same word *for ever* is used of the kindling of the Tabernacle lampstands (Ex. 27:20; Lev. 24:3), of the ceremony of the shewbread (Lev. 24:8), of the service of the brazen laver (Ex. 30:21), of the Levitical Priesthood and Levitical garments (Ex. 28:43; 40:15; Lev. 6:18; 10:9; Num. 10:8; 18:23; 25:13; Deut. 18:5; I Chr. 15:2; 23:13), of the sacrificial system, including the sacrifices and offerings (Ex. 29:28; Lev. 7:34, 36; 10:15; Num. 15:15; 18:8, 11, 19; 19:10), of the Day of Atonement sacrifice (Lev. 16:34), and of the red heifer offering (Num. 19:10).

The last thing to keep in mind is the application: If Sabbath-keeping were mandatory based upon the Hebrew term *for ever*, then so are all the other facets of the Law of Moses. Yet even Sabbath-keepers claim that the Messiah has brought these other things to an end. Therefore, it is inconsistent for them to say that all the others have ended, but the Sabbath has not.

2. Application and Conclusion

If terms such as *for ever, perpetual statute,* and *throughout your generations* mean that the Sabbath is still mandatory, then so are all those other facets of the Law of Moses. Yet even Sabbath-keepers rule out the others but do not rule out the Sabbath, although the same words are used. Thus, they lose their main foundation for arguing of the perpetuity of the Sabbath day. It is inconsistent exegesis to insist on the basis of such terms as *for ever, throughout your generations,* and *perpetual statute* that the Sabbath law is still mandatory, without incorporating all of those other elements from the Law of Moses for the same reason.

G. The Law of Moses Rendered Inoperative

If the Law of Moses has been rendered inoperative, so has the Sabbath. That is precisely the teaching of the New Testament. This is clearly taught in nine passages.

1. The First Eight Passages

a. Romans 7:1-6

Or are ye ignorant, brethren (for I speak to men who know the law), that the law has dominion over a man for so long time as he lives? For the woman that has a husband is bound by law to the husband while he lives; but if the husband die, she is discharged from the law of the husband. So then if, while the husband lives, she be joined to another man, she shall be called an adulteress: but if the husband die, she is free from the law, so that she is no adulteress, though she be joined to another man. Wherefore, my brethren, ye also were made dead to the law through the body of Messiah, that ye should be joined to another, even to him who was raised from the dead, that we might bring forth fruit unto God. For when we were in the flesh, the sinful passions, which were through the law, wrought in our members to bring forth fruit unto death. But now we have been discharged from the law, having died to that wherein we were held; so that we serve in newness of the spirit, and not in oldness of the letter.

When a husband dies, a wife becomes a widow and is no longer bound to "the law of the husband" (vv. 1-3). Therefore, she is free to remarry without committing the sin of adultery; she is now *free from the law*, because a death has taken place. Paul then makes the theological application (vv. 4-6). Here, again, a death has taken place, the death of the Messiah. Believers have been *made dead to the law through the body of Messiah* (v. 4). The sin nature can no longer use the law as a base of operation (v. 5). Finally, Paul states that *we have been discharged from the law* (v. 6). One is either married to the Law or to the Messiah but cannot be married to both.

b. Romans 10:4

For Messiah is the end of the law unto righteousness to every one that believes.

Four things should be noted about this passage. First, the Greek word for *end* is *telos*, which can mean one of two things. Rarely does it mean "goal." This would mean that the Messiah is the goal of the Law. However, the primary meaning is *end* or *termination*, which would mean that the Messiah is the *end* of the Law. The primary meaning always has priority, but in essence both are true. The Messiah is both the "goal of the Law," which the Bible teaches, but He is also *the end of the law*. Second, this is true of all 613 commandments, not just some, including the Sabbath commandment. Third, this means that there is no justification through the Law (Gal. 2:16). And fourth, there is no sanctification through the Law either (Heb. 7:19).

c. Galatians 3:19a

This passage clearly states that the Law was temporary until *the seed should come*:

What then is the law? It was added because of transgressions, till the seed should come to whom the promise has been made; . . .

Six things are noteworthy about this passage. First, the Law was an addition to the Abrahamic Covenant in order to make sin very clear. Second, the Law was temporary until the coming of the Seed, the Messiah. Third, the Messiah has now come, which means the Law is no longer the rule of life. Fourth, the Law was a *tutor* (Gal. 3:24). Fifth, Galatians 3:25 adds that *we are no longer under* [this] *tutor*, we are no longer under the Law. And sixth, we have been redeemed from the Law (Gal. 4:5).

d. Galatians 3:24-25

[24]*So that the law is become our tutor to bring us unto Messiah, that we might be justified by faith.* [25]*But now that faith has come, we are no longer under a tutor*

This passage points out two things: In verse 24, the Law was a *tutor*, meaning "a pedagogue" or "a teacher," whose duty is to bring one to maturity in the Messiah; and in verse 25, the believer is no longer under this *tutor*.

e. Ephesians 2:11-16

Verses 14-15 state:

[14] For he is our peace, who made both one, and broke down the middle wall of partition, [15] having abolished in his flesh the enmity, even the law of commandments contained in ordinances; that he might create in himself of the two one new man, so making peace; . . .

This passage points out two things about our subject: First, in verse 14, the Law was *the middle wall of partition*; and second, *the middle wall of partition* is no more, for it was broken down. In verse 15, it has been abolished.

f. Hebrews 7:11-12, and 18

[11] Now if there was perfection through the Levitical priesthood (for under it has the people received the law), what further need was there that another priest should arise after the order of Melchizedek, and not be reckoned after the order of Aaron? [12] For the priesthood being changed, there is made of necessity a change also of the law.

* * *

[18] For there is a disannulling of a foregoing commandment because of its weakness and unprofitableness . . .

This passage discusses the new priesthood and points out three things: first, in verse 11, that the Messiah is a priest after the Order of Melchizedek, something that the Law of Moses did not allow; second, in verse 12, that a new priesthood required a change of the Law; and third, in verse 18, that the Law of Moses has been disannulled so that the Messiah can function in His new priesthood.

g. Hebrews 8:13

The context of this verse is Hebrews 8:8-13, in which the author explains that the truth of Hebrews 7:11-12 and 18 was already anticipated by the prophets. In verses 8-12, he quotes the New Covenant of Jeremiah 31:31-34 and then concludes in verse 13:

> *In that he says, A new covenant, he has made the first old. But that which is becoming old and waxed aged is nigh unto vanishing away.*

Thus the Law of Moses became *old* with Jeremiah and vanished away with the Messiah's death.

h. II Corinthians 3:2-11

This passage focuses on the one part of the Mosaic Law that most people seem to want to hang on to: the Ten Commandments. It points out four things. First, it states what the Law of Moses was a *ministration of death* in verse 7 and a *ministration of condemnation* in verse 9.

The second thing is that this passage spotlights the Ten Commandments because it focuses on those commandments of Moses which were *engraven on stones* in verses 3 and 7.

The third thing is that in verses 7 and 11, the Law has now passed away. The Greek word that Paul uses here is *katargeo*, which means "to render inoperative." What these two verses are saying is that the Law has been rendered inoperative. This is true of the whole Law, but in this passage especially, it is true of the Ten Commandments.

The fourth thing the apostle points out in verse 11 is that the Law of the Messiah is superior because it will never pass away.

D. R. de Lacey wrote on this passage:

> Second Corinthians represents a very different situation, but one in which Paul is again fighting an attempt to assert the superiority of the law-keeping apostles at Jerusalem. It is in the context of his self-defense that he returns to the contrast between the old covenant and the new, a contrast that enters his mind first through the demand for written credentials (3:1).

These he contrasts with spiritual credentials written on the heart (3:2-3), which he is confident that he can display, for God has made him the minister of a new and spiritual covenant. Here we still find the polemic of Galatians; the old covenant was by implication in letter and not in spirit. The letter can only kill; it was called "the dispensation of death" (3:6-8). Yet even this "came with splendor" (v. 7). It has lost that splendor only in the light of the far greater glory of the "dispensation of the Spirit," which is not evil but fading (vv. 11, 13).[6]

2. Summary and Conclusions

The Law is one single unit comprised of 613 specific commandments. This whole Law has been rendered inoperative; it is no longer in effect. Even the Ten Commandments no longer apply today for reasons to be discussed later in this study on the Sabbath. The Law is still there in the sense that it could be used as a teaching tool to show God's standard of righteousness as well as man's sinfulness and his need for the Messiah. That is the lawful use of the Law (Gal. 3:23-25). But it is no longer the rule of life for the believer, because the believer is no longer under the Law.

3. The Ninth Passage: Matthew 5:17-19

[17]Think not that I came to destroy the law or the prophets: I came not to destroy, but to fulfil. [18]For verily I say unto you, Till heaven and earth pass away, one jot or one tittle shall in no wise pass away from the law, till all things be accomplished. [19]Whosoever therefore shall break one of these least commandments, and shall teach men so, shall be called least in the kingdom of heaven: but whosoever shall do and teach them, he shall be called great in the kingdom of heaven.

People like to use this passage against the above conclusions, because *Yeshua* said that He did not come *to destroy* or to abolish the

---

[6] D. R. de Lacey, "The Sabbath/Sunday Question and the Law in the Pauline Corpus," in *From Sabbath to Lord's Day: A Biblical, Historical and Theological Investigation* (ed. D. A. Carson; Grand Rapids: Zondervan, 1982), 163.

Law, but *to fulfil* it. So they have made this the main passage to maintain the Sabbath law and other features of the Law.

While they emphasize verse 18, they tend to ignore verse 19, which adds: *these least commandments*. In other words, the context of Matthew 5:17-19 is not only concerned with the Sabbath law or only the Ten Commandments or only the major laws, but even the most minute laws, all 613 commandments. When verse 19 adds, *these least commandments*, it includes the entire Law, all 613 commandments.

The Greek word for "fulfill" is *pleiroō*, which is used by Matthew in the sense of fulfilling prophecy, thus bringing that prophecy to an end. In Matthew 1:22-23, he used the term of the prophecy of Isaiah 7:14. He does not mean that Isaiah 7:14 can be fulfilled again in the future, he simply means that it is a fulfillment of prophecy, bringing it to an end.

The word *pleiroō* means the accomplishment of prophecy by fulfilling it, in contrast to its abolishment by failing to fulfill it. The point of Matthew is that the Messiah came to fulfill, not to abolish.

Furthermore, the words of Matthew 5:17-19 were spoken during *Yeshua's* lifetime when the Law was still in effect. As long as He was living, He still had to obey the Law.

Finally, the Law did not end with the coming of *Yeshua*; it ended with His death. It was then that the Law was rendered inoperative.

H. The Ceremonial, Civil, and Moral Distinctions

The problem faced by adherents of mandatory Sabbath-keeping is that even they realize that the major part of the Law of Moses no longer applies. Even the Seventh Day Adventist and the Jewish believer who believes in the obligation of the Law will admit that great parts of the Mosaic Law are simply no longer applicable. Yet, they want to hang on to certain things, such as the Sabbath.

The supposed solution is that they attempt to make distinctions within the Law of Moses in order to apply commandments such as the Sabbath and do away with others. One such distinction is to divide the Law in two main ways. Some separate the Ten Commandments from the other 603 commandments and say the 603 commandments have been done away with, but the Ten Commandments still apply, which, of course, includes the Sabbath. A second way they try to divide it is by making a threefold distinction: ceremonial, civil, and moral. They would claim that the ceremonial and civil commandments have been done away with, but the moral commandments, the moral law, still apply. Since the Sabbath is part of the moral law, therefore, the Sabbath commandment still applies.

This position can be rebutted in three points. First, the Scriptures always view the Law of Moses as a single unit. This is seen by the fact that both the Hebrew and Greek language use the singular word for "law," even though the Law consists of 613 specific commandments. In Hebrew, the word is *torah*, and in Greek the word is *nomos*, both of which are singular.

The second point is that neither the Scriptures nor Rabbinic Judaism ever made such distinctions. One does not find distinctions such as ceremonial, civil, and moral anywhere in the New Testament, anywhere in Scripture, or even in rabbinic theology.

The third point is that James 2:10 states that to break one commandment is to be guilty of breaking the whole Law. The only way that this can be true is on the principle of the unity of the Mosaic Law. If one breaks a civil commandment, he is guilty of breaking the ceremonial and moral law. If he breaks a ceremonial commandment, he is guilty of breaking the civil and moral law. If he breaks a moral commandment, he is guilty of breaking the ceremonial and civil law, because the Bible treats the Law of Moses as a single unit.

Probably the most exhaustive study on the Sabbath in recent times is by several authors who put together *From Sabbath to Lord's Day*. They have come to similar conclusions. D. A. Carson, in his article "Jesus and the Sabbath in the Four Gospels," commenting on Matthew 12:1-8; Mark 2:23-28; and Luke 6:1-5, states:

> In Sabbatarian apologetic, it is common to distinguish between moral, ceremonial, and civil law. The Sabbath commandment is thought to be binding on all, not only because it is alleged to be a "creation ordinance," but also because it is part of the Decalogue, which is classified as "moral." The distinction

between moral, ceremonial, and civil law is apt, especially in terms of functional description, but it is not self-evident that either the Old Testament or New Testament writers neatly classify Old Testament law in those categories in such a way as to establish continuity and discontinuity on the basis of such distinctions. Even if such categories are applied, it should be noted that both David's lawbreaking and that of the priests (found only in Matthew) come from ceremonial law. It is difficult, then, to resist the conclusion that their applicability to the Sabbath case puts Sabbath law in the ceremonial category with them.

... It must be insisted that to read such categories back into Matthew 5:17-20 and conclude that only moral law is in view would be anachronistic. This is not to deny that Jesus himself makes no distinctions whatsoever in Old Testament law, nor to say that the distinctions are always invalid. Rather it is to say that the New Testament writers do not in any case appear to establish patterns of continuity or discontinuity on the basis of such distinction. Certainly the phrase "an iota or a dot" excludes any interpretation of the passage that claims that only the "moral law" is in view. [7]

In the same volume, Max Turner wrote in his article "The Sabbath, Sunday, and the Law in Luke/Acts":

... Even less that he (or Luke) operated with such categories as "moral," "ceremonial" and "civil" law, dividing some that are retained from others that are abolished. Indeed, to bring such categories into the discussion at this point would be anachronistic. Jesus fulfills and supersedes the law.[8]

---

[7] D. A. Carson, "Jesus and the Sabbath in the Four Gospels," in *From Sabbath to Lord's Day: A Biblical, Historical and Theological Investigation* (ed. D. A. Carson; Grand Rapids: Zondervan, 1982), 68-9, 78-9.

[8] M. Max B. Turner, "The Sabbath, Sunday, and the Law in Luke/Acts," in *From Sabbath to Lord's Day: A Biblical, Historical and Theological Investigation* (ed. D. A. Carson; Grand Rapids: Zondervan, 1982), 111.

A. T. Lincoln of Gordon-Conwell Seminary, in his chapter, "From Sabbath to Lord's Day: A Biblical and Theological Perspective," states:

> In all of his discussion and terminology, Paul treats the Law of Moses as a total package and makes no distinction between moral and ceremonial elements within.[9]

The application is this: There is simply no biblical validity in distinguishing between ceremonial, civil, and moral parts of the Mosaic Law in order to make some portions of it continue and others not, just to include the Sabbath in those sections that are still obligatory, especially for Jewish believers.

I. The Moral Law and the Law of Moses

What is the relationship of the moral law to the Law of Moses? This question is important because 'Mandatory Sabbath-keepers' like to claim that the moral law was part of the Mosaic Law. They say that since the moral law has continued and since the Sabbath is part of the moral law, it is therefore mandatory.

Concerning the relationship of the moral law and the Law of Moses, several points can be made. The moral law, by way of definition, is those eternal principles of God which reflect His nature. It is true that this law did not terminate at Calvary with the death of the Messiah. However, the moral law did not begin with the Law of Moses on Sinai; it existed as long as there have been moral creatures. Adam and Eve, for example, broke the moral law before Moses. Satan broke the moral law even before Adam and Eve.

The moral law is not the same as the Ten Commandments nor is it equivalent to the Mosaic Law. The Law of Moses included the moral law along with ceremonial commandments, civil laws, criminal laws, sanitary laws, and governmental laws. The moral law existed before Moses and continues beyond and after the cross. What the Ten Commandments

---

[9] A. T. Lincoln, "From Sabbath to Lord's Day: A Biblical and Theological Perspective," in *From Sabbath to Lord's Day: A Biblical, Historical and Theological Investigation* (ed. D. A. Carson; Grand Rapids: Zondervan, 1982), 370.

THE SABBATH

forbade did not begin with Moses except for the Sabbath command, which is far more ceremonial than moral. It was always morally wrong to murder, to steal, and to commit adultery. So while the Law of Moses embodied or incorporated the moral law, it did not originate it.

Today the moral law is embodied in the Law of the Messiah. This does not mean that it is a part of the Mosaic Law that has continued to our day.

J. Is the Sabbath Law Moral or Ceremonial?

A second question arises: Is the Sabbath law moral or ceremonial? The 'Mandatory Sabbath-keepers' insist that the Sabbath law is part of the moral law, and therefore, it is still mandatory today.

The assumption that the Sabbath law is a moral law leads to the conclusion that those who do not keep the Sabbath become immoral. Are Sabbath adherents willing to follow the logic of their position? If they are, they should classify all non-Sabbath-keepers as being guilty of immorality. Furthermore, are they keeping the Sabbath the very way the Law commanded? Or, are they keeping the Sabbath by way of various traditions, such as making it a day of worship rather than a day of rest? If Sabbath adherents are not keeping the Sabbath the same way God commanded in the Law, then they are not keeping the Law, and therefore, they, too, become immoral.

The simple truth is that the Sabbath is not a moral commandment. The Law of Moses treats the Sabbath law as a ceremonial commandment, not as a moral commandment. A moral commandment means it is always wrong. Murder, theft, and adultery are always wrong no matter what day of the week you commit these crimes. However, the very things that were forbidden to be done on the Sabbath day were permitted to be done on the other days. This clearly shows that the Sabbath commandment was not a moral commandment, but a ceremonial commandment. If, then, the ceremonial law has been done away with, it means that the Sabbath was also done away with, because the Sabbath is treated by Scripture not as a moral commandment, but as a ceremonial commandment.

K. Conclusion

Not only is there no basis for mandatory Sabbath-keeping based upon the Sabbath being a creation ordinance, there can also be no valid grounds for mandatory Sabbath-keeping from the Law of Moses. It has been shown that no argument used to support mandatory Sabbath-keeping on the basis of the Law of Moses has been substantiated.

De Lacey gives an excellent summary of Law and its applicability today:

> The law presents mankind with the ethical standards of the holy God. As such, its goodness is unquestionable, but its effect is simply to demonstrate the existence of our sin, to condemn us as a result, and also to provoke our sin. Because of the weakness of the flesh, it can have no other effect on us when we read its righteous demands. Only death with Christ will remove us from the condemnation that it would otherwise constantly pronounce on anyone who endeavored to live by its standards.
>
> But the law also stands for the whole covenantal arrangement that God made with His people at Sinai, a covenant that has now manifestly been replaced by the New Covenant in Christ. In both of these aspects, Paul realized that the law no longer played any role in the life of a Christian. His new and Christian insights into the "exceeding sinfulness of sin" also led him to see that any attempt, even by Christians, to use the law as a basis for a standing before God led inevitably to the sin of "boasting," that is, faith in self rather than faith in God. The only Christian way to fulfill one's obligation to God is by fulfilling the law of love (the law of subordinating one's own self to the other), by walking in the Spirit. These two factors, love and the Spirit, Paul sees as keeping Christian obedience

from degenerating into formal legalism. Too rarely, alas, has the church been able to preserve this Pauline insight.[10]

---

[10] D. R. de Lacey, "The Sabbath/Sunday Question and the Law in the Pauline Corpus," in *From Sabbath to Lord's Day: A Biblical, Historical and Theological Investigation* (ed. D. A. Carson; Grand Rapids: Zondervan, 1982), 175.

V. THE SABBATH IN THE PROPHETS

The previous category dealt with the Sabbath in the Law. This chapter will deal with the Sabbath in the Prophets in two main sections: First, some passages in the Prophets which speak of the Sabbath will be surveyed; and second, some observations and conclusions will be drawn.

A. The Passages

All together there are eighteen passages in this section of the study of the Sabbath in the Prophets.

1. II Kings 4:23

This passage deals with the issue of inquiring of a prophet on a Sabbath day. The verse has the husband of the Shunammite woman asking her: *Wherefore will you go to him* [Elisha] *to-day? it is neither new moon nor sabbath.* The Shunammite woman was going to Elisha to request the life of her son who had just died. The passing comment made by her husband shows that there was a custom of going to inquire of a prophet on the Sabbath day, as well as on the New Moon day.

2. II Kings 11:5, 7, and 9

⁵And he commanded them, saying, This is the thing that ye shall do: a third part of you, that come in on the sabbath, shall be keepers of the watch of the king's house;...

* * *

⁷And the two companies of you, even all that go forth on the sabbath, shall keep the watch of the house of Jehovah about the king.

* * *

⁹And the captains over hundreds did according to all that Jehoiada the priest commanded; and they took every man his men, those that were to come in on the sabbath, with those that were to go out on the sabbath, and came to Jehoiada the priest.

The context of these verses is the overthrow of Queen Athaliah. The point here is that Athaliah was deposed on a Sabbath day. Jehoiadah, the high priest, used the regular Sabbath procedure of changing the Levitical guard as a subterfuge to spring his plan.

3. II Kings 16:18

And the covered way for the sabbath that they had built in the house, and the king's entry without, turned he unto the house of Jehovah, because of the king of Assyria.

This passage has to do with something Solomon built, called *the covered way for the sabbath*. We are not sure what this was referring to. It may have been a colonnade in the Temple Compound or it may have been a covered place or a covered stand or a covered hole in the Court of the Temple. Whatever it was, the king used it whenever he visited the Temple.

4. Isaiah 1:13

Bring no more vain oblations; incense is an abomination unto me; new moon and sabbath, the calling of assemblies, - I cannot away with iniquity and the solemn meeting.

Here God speaks through Isaiah about the Sabbath offerings and orders a cessation of the bringing of the sacrifices for the Sabbath. This was not a cancellation of the Mosaic Law, but it was a condemnation of ritual without reality; the sacrifices offered for the Sabbath in accordance with the Law of Moses were nothing more than mere externalism by this time.

5. Isaiah 56:1-8

This is a prophetic passage dealing with the Sabbath in the Messianic Kingdom. The key verses are 2, 4, and 6.

[2]Blessed is the man that...keeps the sabbath from profaning it, . . .

* * *

⁴For thus says Jehovah of the eunuchs that keep my sabbaths, ...

* * *

⁶Also the foreigners...every one that keep the sabbath from profaning it, ...

Contextually, this passage deals with the observance of the Sabbath in the Temple in the Messianic Kingdom, the Millennium. It points out two things. First, the Sabbath will be kept by *the eunuchs*, whose entry into the Temple Compound was forbidden by the Law of Moses, but will be permitted under Millennial Law. Second, the foreigners or Gentiles, whose entry was also forbidden into the Temple Compound by the Law of Moses, but will be permitted by Millennial Law, will keep it.

6. Isaiah 58:13

If you turn away your foot from the sabbath, from doing your pleasure on my holy day; and call the sabbath a delight, and the holy of Jehovah honorable; and shall honor it, ...

The verse gives four different descriptions concerning the Sabbath: First, it is *a delight*; second, it is *my holy day*, meaning God's holy day; third, it is *the holy of Jehovah*; and fourth, it is *honorable*. He then promised a blessing if one would honor the Sabbath.

This passage is an admonition for the Jews of Isaiah's day to keep the Sabbath based upon the Mosaic Law. The admonition has both a negative and a positive feature. Negatively, one is not to *turn away* [his] *foot*, for to profane the Sabbath is to do one's own pleasure on the Sabbath. Positively, one is to *honor it* by keeping it in accordance with the Law of Moses.

7. Isaiah 66:23

And it shall come to pass, from one new moon to another, and from one sabbath to another, shall all flesh come to worship before me, says Jehovah.

This passage deals with the Sabbath in the Kingdom. Sabbath-keeping will be mandatory in the Messianic Kingdom for both Jews and Gentiles. All will come to worship God in Jerusalem on the Sabbath day.

8. Jeremiah 17:21-27

This passage is an admonition to keep the Sabbath in Jeremiah's day, just as Isaiah admonished the Jewish people to keep the Sabbath in his day. Verses 21-22 state:

> *²¹Thus says Jehovah, Take heed to yourselves, and bear no burden on the sabbath day, nor bring it in by the gates of Jerusalem; ²²neither carry forth a burden out of your houses on the sabbath day, neither do ye any work: but hallow ye the sabbath day, as I commanded your fathers.*

Verse 23 points out that the fathers disobeyed the Sabbath commandment. Verse 24 states:

> *And it shall come to pass, if* [they] *diligently hearken* [to God]*, to bring in no burden through the gates of the city on the sabbath day, but to hallow the sabbath day, to do no work therein; . . .*

The results will be twofold: First, in verse 25, one result will be that the city will have peace and prosperity; the second result will be that Jews from all areas will bring their sacrifices to Jerusalem, according to verse 26.

However, verse 27 warns them of what might happen if they will not listen to God:

> *But if ye will not hearken unto me to hallow the sabbath day, and not to bear a burden and enter in at the gates of Jerusalem on the sabbath day; then will I kindle a fire in the gates thereof, and it shall devour the palaces of Jerusalem, and it shall not be quenched.*

The way to *not hearken* to God is to fail to hallow the Sabbath day, bearing a burden and entering the gates of Jerusalem on the Sabbath day. The result will be the destruction of Jerusalem.

This admonition to keep the Sabbath day is based upon the Law of Moses. The command proper includes the following: to carry no burden into Jerusalem on the Sabbath day; to carry no burden out of their houses on the Sabbath day; to do no work on the Sabbath day; and to hallow or sanctify the Sabbath. While obedience will bring peace and blessing as the Law of Moses itself had promised, disobedience will bring the destruction of Jerusalem.

9. Ezekiel 20:12-24

This passage is a review of the Sabbath in Israel's history. Verse 12 states:

Moreover also I gave them my sabbaths [for two reasons: first], *to be a sign between me and them,* [and second] *that they might know that I am Jehovah that sanctifies them.*

Verse 13 points out: *my sabbaths they greatly profaned.* The result was that God poured out His wrath upon them in the wilderness. According to verse 14, it was in this way that God's name was profaned. The punishment, in verse 15, was that they were not to be allowed to enter the Land. In verse 16, the reason was that they profaned His Sabbaths; they failed to keep the Sabbath even in the wilderness. Nevertheless, in verse 17, God did spare them as a nation.

In verse 18, there is a warning not to walk after their fathers. But in verse 19, they are to keep His commandments. In verse 20, they are to specifically *hallow my sabbaths* for two reasons: First, the Sabbath is a *sign between me and you*; and second: *that ye may know that I am Jehovah your God.*

In verse 21, however, Israel profaned His Sabbaths, and the result was punishment in the wilderness; however, in verse 22, the punishment was not total. In verse 23, there was now a threat of dispersion, and in verse 24, the reason was that they had *profaned my sabbaths.*

Four things should be noted from this passage. First, it contains a summary of Israel's disobedience in the wilderness, which includes the profaning of the Sabbath. Second, the Sabbath is a sign of two things: that it is God who sanctifies Israel; and that it is Jehovah who is Israel's God. Third, He refers to the Sabbath as *my sabbaths*, and so God claims the Sabbath as His own. Fourth, the command proper was to *hallow my sabbaths*.

10. Ezekiel 22:8

You have despised my holy things, and have profaned my sabbaths.

This passage deals with the princes of Judah and their relationship to the Sabbath; they had profaned God's Sabbaths. Two points are made: First, the civil leadership of Israel was guilty in Ezekiel's day of violating the Sabbath commandment; and second, the violation of the Sabbath commandment was a violation under the Law of Moses.

11. Ezekiel 22:26

Her priests have done violence to my law, and have profaned my holy things: they have made no distinction between the holy and the common, neither have they caused men to discern between the unclean and the clean, and have hid their eyes from my sabbaths, and I am profaned among them.

This passage deals with the relationship of the priests and the Sabbath day: they *have hid their eyes from my sabbaths*. Just as the civil leadership the princes, so the religious leadership of Israel of Ezekiel's day had also violated the Sabbath. This violation of the Sabbath commandment was a violation under the Law of Moses.

12. Ezekiel 23:38

Moreover this they have done unto me; they have defiled my sanctuary in the same day, and have profaned my sabbaths.

This twelfth passage deals with the two houses of Israel and the Sabbath. The verse points out that they *have profaned my sabbaths*; both houses of Israel were guilty of violating the Sabbath commandment under the Law of Moses.

13. Ezekiel 44:24

And in a controversy they shall stand to judge; according to mine ordinances shall they judge it; and they shall keep my laws and my statues in all my appointed feasts; and they shall hallow my sabbaths.

This passage deals with the Sabbath in the Messianic Kingdom. The prophecy is: *they shall hallow my sabbaths.*

This verse teaches two things: In the future Messianic Kingdom, Israel will be characterized by keeping the Sabbath. The Sabbath, therefore, will be mandatory in the Kingdom.

14. Ezekiel 45:17

And it shall be the prince's part to give the burnt-offerings, and the meal offerings, and the drink-offerings, in the feasts, and on the new moons, and on the sabbaths, . . .

This passage also deals with the Sabbath in the Kingdom. Two things come out in this verse: First, the Sabbath in the Kingdom will be observed with special offerings; second, once again, the Sabbath will be mandatory in the Kingdom.

15. Ezekiel 46:1-5

This passage again deals with the observance of the Sabbath in the Millennial Kingdom.

Verse 1 mentions the *gate of the inner court that looks toward the east,* meaning the Eastern Gate of the inner court, is going to be shut for *the six working days,* but it will be open *on the sabbath day.* It will also be open *on the day of the new moon.*

Verse 2 deals with *the prince* and with the Inner Eastern Gate.

Verse 3 points out that *the people of the land shall worship* God at this gate in the future on two occasions: *on the sabbaths and on the new moons*, which is the first of every month.

Verse 4 deals with the burnt-offerings for the Sabbath day, which consist of *six lambs without blemish and one ram without blemish*.

Verse 5 mentions two other offerings: first, *the meal-offering*, which will consist of *an ephah for the ram, and the meal-offering for the lambs as he is able to give*; and second, *a hin of oil to an ephah*.

Four truths are found in this passage concerning the Sabbath in the Prophets. First, it deals with the Sabbath and the law of the Inner Eastern Gate of the Temple Compound in the Millennium: This gate will be shut during the six working days, but it will be opened on the Sabbath day. Second, the people will worship God before this gate on the Sabbath. Third, concerning the Sabbath and sacrifices, there will be special sacrifices on the Sabbath day in the Kingdom as there were special sacrifices on the Sabbath day under the Law of Moses, but these sacrifices are different from those of the Law of Moses. There will be a sacrificial system in the Kingdom, but it will not be a reinstitution of the Mosaic system; it is going to be a new system based upon Millennial Law, Kingdom Law, not Mosaic Law. Fourth, the Sabbath will be mandatory in the Kingdom.

16. Ezekiel 46:12

And when the prince shall prepare a freewill-offering,...one shall open for him the gate that looks toward the east; and he shall prepare his burnt-offering and his peace-offerings, as he does on the sabbath day; . . .

This passage deals with the Sabbath observance in the Kingdom. The verse points out that *the prince* – meaning King David – will prepare other offerings as he does on the Sabbath day.

Two observations can be made in this verse: The Sabbath will be a day of special sacrifices, and Sabbath observance will be mandatory in the Messianic Kingdom.

17. Hosea 2:11

I will also cause all her mirth to cease, her feasts, her new moons, and her sabbaths, and all her solemn assemblies.

This passage contains a prophecy for the cessation of the Sabbath: God will *cause all her* (meaning Israel's) *mirth to cease.* Among the things He will cause to cease include: *her feasts, her new moons, and her sabbaths, and all her solemn assemblies.* This verse is a prediction of a future cessation of the Sabbath.

The question is: When was this fulfilled, if it was? First of all, it was not fulfilled during the Dispensation of the Law because the Sabbath was still mandatory throughout the entire period of the Law. Second, it will not be true in the Dispensation of the Kingdom for, according to the prophecies of both Isaiah and Ezekiel, the Sabbath will be mandatory in the Messianic Kingdom. Third, this can only be true for the present Dispensation of Grace. Today, the Sabbath has ceased; it is no longer mandatory. The reason is because the Sabbath is not part of the Law of the Messiah. It is a fulfillment of the prophecy of Hosea 2:11, predicting a cessation of the Sabbath.

18. Amos 8:5

. . . When will the new moon be gone, that we may sell grain? And the sabbath, that we may set forth wheat, making the ephah small, and the shekel great, and dealing falsely with balances of deceit;

This final passage also deals with disobedience of the Sabbath law under the Mosaic Law. The merchants were anxious for the Sabbath to end so as to be able to engage in business. This, too, speaks of violation of the Sabbath law under the Mosaic Law.

B. Observations and Conclusions

Concerning the Sabbath in the Prophets, the first observation is that the prophets gave two specific commands on what was forbidden to do on the Sabbath: There was to be no burden-bearing (Jer. 17:21) and no trading (Amos 8:5).

The second observation is that the Sabbath is *a sign* (Ezek. 20:12, 20). According to verse 12, it was a sign that it is Jehovah who sanctifies Israel. In verse 20, it is the sign that Jehovah is Israel's God.

The third observation is that the Prophets gave four descriptions of the Sabbath, which are all found in Isaiah 58:13: It was God's *holy day*, a *delight*, *the holy of Jehovah*, and it was *honorable*. The verse described it as "a day of gladness."

The fourth observation is that Israel's history is characterized by violating the Sabbath according to the prophets (Is. 1:13; Ezek. 20:12-24; 22:8, 26; 23:38; Amos 8:5).

The fifth observation is that there were, however, prophetic admonitions to keep the Sabbath (Is. 58:13; Jer. 17:21-27).

And the sixth observation is that there were prophecies concerning the Sabbath. According to Hosea 2:11, it was destined to cease for a long period of time, which is the age in which we now live. But it is to be re-instituted in the Kingdom. Isaiah 56:1-8 states that it will be kept by both Jews and Gentiles in the Temple Compound. According to Isaiah 66:23, both Jews and Gentiles will worship God in Jerusalem on the Sabbath day. Ezekiel 44:24 teaches that Israel will then be characterized by keeping the Sabbath. Ezekiel 45:17 states that the Sabbath will be observed with special sacrifices. Ezekiel 46:1-5 points out that these sacrifices will be offered at the Inner Eastern Gate by *the prince*, King David; these sacrifices will be different from those of the Mosaic Law; and it will be the only day of the week when the Inner Eastern Gate will be open. Finally, Ezekiel 46:12 deals, again, with *the prince*, King David, who will be in charge of the sacrifices.

VI. THE SABBATH IN THE WRITINGS

This chapter will discuss the Sabbath in the Writings, the third division of the Hebrew Old Testament. This, too, will be dealt with in two sections: first, the key passages; and second, some observations and conclusions.

A. Key Passages

All together there are twelve passages in the Writings which speak of the Sabbath.

1. I Chronicles 9:32

And some of their brethren, of the sons of the Kohathites, were over the showbread, to prepare it every sabbath.

This passage, which deals with the preparation of the shewbread on the Sabbath day, tells us three things: The shewbread had to be changed every Sabbath according to the Law of Moses. The division of the Tribe of Levi that had this responsibility was the Kohathites. Finally, this was in keeping with the ceremonial facet of the Sabbath law.

2. I Chronicles 23:31

... and to offer all burnt-offerings unto Jehovah, on the sabbaths, on the new moons, and on the set feasts, in number according to the ordinance concerning them, continually before Jehovah; ...

This second passage deals with the burnt-offerings. According to the Law of Moses, the Sabbath required special sacrifices. The Levites were assigned to carry them out. This too was in keeping with the ceremonial facet of the Law of Moses.

3. II Chronicles 2:4

The third passage spells out the purpose of the Temple, which included the sacrifice of burnt-offerings *on the sabbaths, and on the new moons, and on the set feasts.*

Two observations can be made: First, the Temple was now to be the place for the Sabbath sacrifices, replacing the Tabernacle; and second, this, too, was in keeping with the ceremonial aspect of the Mosaic Law.

4. II Chronicles 8:13

> *... even as the duty of every day required, offering according to the commandment of Moses, on the sabbaths, and on the new moons, and on the set feasts, three times in the year, even in the feast of unleavened bread, and in the feast of weeks, and in the feast of tabernacles.*

The fourth passage deals with Solomon's observance of the Sabbath. It reiterates that the Law of Moses required special sacrifices for the Sabbath. Solomon made sure that these offerings were provided in keeping with the Law; and, again, this was in keeping with the ceremonial facet of the Law of Moses.

5. II Chronicles 31:2-3

The fifth passage deals with Hezekiah and the Sabbath. Verse 3 states:

> *He appointed also the king's portion of his substance for the burnt-offerings ... for the sabbaths, and for the new moons, and for the set feasts, as it is written in the law of Jehovah.*

Three observations can be made from this passage. First, the Law of Moses required special sacrifices for the Sabbath. Second, like Solomon, Hezekiah the king made sure that the offerings were provided in keeping with the Law. And third, this was in keeping with the ceremonial facet of the Law of Moses.

6. Nehemiah 9:14

... and made known to them your holy sabbath, and commanded them commandments, and statutes, and a law, by Moses your servant.

The sixth passage deals with the Sabbath as a Mosaic commandment. The verse states that God made known to Israel His *holy sabbath* at Mount Sinai.

This is a reference to the origin of the observance of the Sabbath commandment given at Sinai. By stating *your holy sabbath*, it points out that this is God's Sabbath, it is God's holy day.

7. Nehemiah 10:31

The seventh passage deals with the covenant to keep the Law:

... and if the peoples of the land bring wares or any grain on the sabbath day to sell, that we would not buy of them on the sabbath, or on a holy day; and that we would forego the seventh year, and the extraction of every debt.

Two observations can be made in this verse: First, the command proper is that there is to be no marketing on the Sabbath day; and second, the Jews of the return from Babylon committed themselves to keep the Sabbath in accordance with the Law of Moses.

8. Nehemiah 10:33

The eighth passage deals with the Temple tax and the Sabbath. The verse mentions *for the sabbaths*.

Again, we can make two observations: The Jews who returned from Babylon agreed to pay the Temple tax to finance Temple functions, which included the Sabbath functions. This too was in keeping with the ceremonial facet of the Sabbath law.

9. Nehemiah 13:15-22

The ninth passage deals with disobedience to the Sabbath law. Verses 15-18 state:

> *[15]In those days saw I in Judah some men treading wine-presses on the sabbath, and bringing in sheaves, and lading asses therewith; as also wine, grapes, and figs, and all manner of burdens, which they brought into Jerusalem on the sabbath day: and I testified against them in the day wherein they sold victuals. [16]There dwelt men of Tyre also therein, who brought in fish, and all manner of wares, and sold on the sabbath unto the children of Judah, and in Jerusalem. [17]Then I contended with the nobles of Judah, and said unto them, What evil thing is this that ye do, and profane the sabbath day? [18]Did not your fathers thus, and did not our God bring all the evil upon us, and upon this city? yet ye bring more wrath upon Israel by profaning the sabbath.*

There are seven things to note in this passage. First, in verse 15, the passage records the violation of the Sabbath by the Jews of the return from Babylon. The second thing to note is that this was the violation of the Sabbath under the Law of Moses. Third, they were guilty of profaning the Sabbath in six ways: treading grapes, carrying sheaves, loading asses, carrying burdens, marketing, and buying. In verse 16, the fourth thing to note is that *men of Tyre*, Gentiles, would market on the Sabbath day, but the Jews would buy from them, which was also forbidden for the Sabbath. In verse 17, the fifth observation is that the nobles or Jewish leaders condoned this profaning of the Sabbath. And in verse 18, the sixth thing to note is that Nehemiah warned that a continuation of profaning the Sabbath would bring on the wrath of God.

The seventh observation is that Nehemiah took four countermeasures in verses 19-22:

> *[19]And it came to pass that, when the gates of Jerusalem began to be dark before the sabbath, I commanded that the doors should be shut, and commanded that they should not be opened till after the sabbath: and some of my servants set I over the gates, that there should no burden be brought in on*

the sabbath day. ²⁰So the merchants and sellers of all kinds of wares lodged without Jerusalem once or twice. ²¹Then I testified against them, and said unto them, Why lodge ye about the wall? if ye do so again, I will lay hands on you. From that time forth came they no more on the sabbath. ²²And I commanded the Levites that they should purify themselves, and that they should come and keep the gates, to sanctify the sabbath day. Remember unto me, O my God, this also, and spare me according to the greatness of your lovingkindness.

Because the people profaned the Sabbath in so many ways, Nehemiah decided to take action. The first countermeasure, in verse 19, is that on Friday evenings the gates were shut and not reopened until after the Sabbath on Saturday evening. The second countermeasure, in verse 19, is that the servants of Nehemiah were placed as guardians of the gates to make sure no one brought a burden into Jerusalem. The third countermeasure, in verses 20-21, is that the Gentile merchants who tried to sleep outside the walls were warned against doing so in the future. And the fourth countermeasure, in verse 22, is that the Levites were ordered to guard the gates to keep the Sabbath from being profaned and to become examples of Sabbath-keeping themselves.

10. Psalm 92: Superscription

The superscription, the little title found under the number of Psalm 92 before the first verse, states: *A Psalm, a Song for the sabbath day.* This was a psalm written to be sung on the Sabbath day. While many of the other psalms may have been written for the same reason, this is the only one that is actually stated to be for that purpose. As a whole, the psalm is a praise of God's goodness.

There are five rabbinic interpretations of this psalm. One rabbi said that this was a psalm for the age to come, the Messianic Kingdom. A second rabbi said that this psalm describes the age to come, which will be entirely Sabbath. A third rabbi said something similar: "The day which is entirely Sabbath." A fourth rabbi said that this is a psalm for the age to come, for the day which will be entirely Sabbath and rest in eternal life. And the fifth rabbi said that this is a psalm for the day which is entirely Sabbath, in which there is no eating or drinking, no buying or selling, but men will sit with their crowns on their heads and refresh themselves in the splendor in the *Shechinah* Glory.

11. Lamentations 1:7

Jerusalem remembered in the days of her affliction and of her miseries all her pleasant things that were from the days of old: When her people fell into the hand of the adversary, and none did help her, the Adversaries saw her, they did mock at her desolations.

The Hebrew word translated as *desolations* literally should be *ceasings* (as can be seen in the ASV margin), and the actual word means *from her sabbaths*. This eleventh passage points out that the Babylonians mocked the way the Jews observed the Sabbath at the time when the Temple was destroyed in 586 B.C.

12. Lamentations 2:6

And he has violently taken away is tabernacle, as if it were of a garden; he has destroyed his place of assembly: Jehovah has caused solemn assembly and sabbath to be forgotten in Zion, And has despised in the indignation of his anger the king and the priest.

The twelfth passage deals with the fall of Jerusalem in the year 586 B.C. When that happened, *Jehovah has caused solemn assembly and sabbath to be forgotten in Zion*. This verse points out the cessation of the Sabbath observance in the Temple Compound as a result of the Babylonian destruction of the Temple in 586 B.C.

B. Observations and Conclusions

After studying the Sabbath in the Writings, we can draw seven observations and conclusions. First, there were three specific commandments for the Sabbath day: There was to be no marketing, no burden-bearing, and no labor. This "no labor" commandment itself included three things: no treading of grapes, no carrying of sheaves, and no loading of asses or donkeys.

Second, there was a reaffirmation that the Sabbath was given by God to Moses at Mount Sinai.

Third, the Sabbath was God's Sabbath; He claimed it as His own.

Fourth, the Writings had a heavy emphasis on the ceremonial facets of the Sabbath. For example, I Chronicles 9:32 spoke of the shewbread on the Sabbath; I Chronicles 23:31 described the burnt-offerings on the Sabbath; II Chronicles 2:4, stated that this was the purpose of the Temple and that the Temple was built to expedite the Sabbath observance as far as sacrifices are concerned; II Chronicles 8:12-13 spoke about Solomon's provisions for Sabbath sacrifices; II Chronicles 31:2-3 spoke of Hezekiah's provisions; and finally, Nehemiah 10:33 spoke about the Temple tax for the purpose of providing sacrifices for the Sabbath.

Fifth, the Jews of the return from Babylon committed themselves to keep the Sabbath in Nehemiah 10:31 and 33.

Sixth, they quickly fell into disobedience in Nehemiah 13:15-22.

Seventh, Psalm 92 was a special psalm that was composed to be sung on the Sabbath day.

VII. THE SABBATH IN THE NEW TESTAMENT

The seventh chapter of the study of the Sabbath is divided into five sections and will look at the Sabbath in the Gospels, in the Book of Acts, in the Epistles of Paul, and in the Book of Hebrews. In the final section, we will summarize the findings and draw certain conclusions.

A. The Sabbath in the Gospels

To understand the controversial issues between *Yeshua* and the Pharisees, it is necessary to look at the historical background as to how Pharisaic Judaism developed. When the Jewish people returned from the Babylonian Captivity, the spiritual leaders recognized that the reason for the captivity had been disobedience to the Mosaic Law. Ezra began a school called the School of the *Sopherim* or the School of the Scribes. Their plan was to go through each of the 613 commandments God gave to Moses and expound them to the Jewish people. Their thinking was that, by giving them a clear knowledge of what the Law was and how to keep it, they would not bring on another divine discipline like the Babylonian Captivity.

When the first generation of the *Sopherim* passed away, the second generation took the task more seriously, saying, "It is not enough for us to expound the Law; we must build a fence around the Law." The fence they built consisted of new rules and regulations logically derived from the original 613 commandments. The principle they used was: A *sopher* may disagree with a *sopher*, but he may not disagree with the *Torah*, which was sacrosanct. Therefore, there was no basis for denying the validity of that Law. In making these new rules and regulations, they could disagree among themselves until they reached a decision by majority vote. Once a decision was reached, it became mandatory for all Jews everywhere in the world to follow. The period of the *Sopherim* began around 450 B.C. and ended in 30 B.C.

After that, a second school of rabbis developed called the *Tannaim*, meaning "teachers." The *Tannaim* looked upon the work of the *Sopherim* and declared, "There are still too many holes in this fence." They continued the process for a period of two hundred and fifty years, from 30 B.C. until A.D. 220. However, the principle of operation changed. The new principle was: A *tanna* may disagree with a *tanna*, but he may not disagree with a *sopher*. This meant that from 30 B.C. onward, all the thousands of rules and regulations passed down by the *Sopherim* became sacrosanct and of equal validity with Scripture.

In order to validate to the Jewish audience why the laws of the *Sopherim* were equal to the laws of Moses, they came up with a teaching that all Orthodox Jews believe and teach to this very day. Their teaching was that what really happened on Mount Sinai was that God gave Moses two laws: the Written Law and the Oral Law. The first law is called the Written Law because it contains the 613 commandments that Moses actually penned in the Books of Exodus, Leviticus, Numbers, and Deuteronomy. The second law is called the Oral Law because Moses did not write down those commandments; he memorized them all. By memory, they were passed down to Joshua, who then passed them down to the Judges, who then passed them down to the Prophets, who then passed them down to the *Sopherim*. So the *Sopherim* did not really innovate all these rules and regulations; they got them from the Prophets, who got them from the Judges, who got them from Joshua, who got them from Moses, who got them from God. Indeed, from about 450 B.C. until A.D. 220, these rules were never written down. Key rabbis and scribes had them memorized, and thousands and thousands of laws were kept strictly on the basis of memory. They were not written down for about six centuries. By A.D. 220, fewer and fewer people were around to memorize all these laws, so they finally wrote them all down at the order of Judah Ha-Nasi, the patriarch in the Land. This ended the period of the *Tannaim*.

The work of the *Sopherim* and the *Tannaim* together is now called the *Mishnah*. It is the *Mishnah* that became the cause of controversy between *Yeshua* and the Pharisees. The Pharisaic concept of the Messiah was that He would be a Pharisee; He would be in submission to the laws of the *Mishnah*; in fact, He would join them in the work of making new laws to plug up the holes in the fence. A Messiah who was not a Pharisee under the *Mishnah's* authority could not possibly be the true Messiah. Any time the terms Mishnaic Law, Pharisaic Law, Rabbinic Law, or Oral Law are used, they refer to the body of material now known as the *Mishnah*. In the New Testament, these laws are called the tradition of the elders. While the Messiah and the Pharisees debated over the authority of the *Mishnah* in general, one specific area of debate was on the proper way of observing the Sabbath.

1. The Sabbath Events

All together there are thirteen Sabbath experiences or events in the Gospels. We will look at each one of them and give the basic content of these passages before drawing final conclusions.

a. The First Visit to Nazareth

The first recorded Sabbath experience was *Yeshua's* first visit to Nazareth in Luke 4:16-30, especially verse 16:

> *And he came to Nazareth, where he had been brought up: and he entered, as his custom was, into the synagogue on the sabbath day, and stood up to read.*

On this Sabbath day, He claimed to be the Messiah in the synagogue of his own hometown of Nazareth, but that led to a quick rejection.

b. Authority over Demons

The second Sabbath experience, found in two of the Gospels, was one in which He showed His authority over demons. First, in Mark 1:21-28, especially verse 21:

> *And they go into Capernaum; and straightway on the sabbath day he entered into the synagogue and taught.*

This verse reveals that as *Yeshua* was teaching in the synagogue of Capernaum. He was teaching authoritatively, not as the Scribes. He then showed His authority over demons by casting them out.

The second passage of the same event is in Luke 4:31-37, especially verse 31:

> *And he came down to Capernaum, a city of Galilee. And he was teaching them on the sabbath day: . . .*

This verse also points out that He was teaching in the synagogue on the Sabbath day; the Jewish response was astonishment at the content of His teaching, His speaking; His teaching was with authority. He then showed His authority by casting out demons.

c. The Healing of the Paralytic

The third Sabbath event is in John 5:1-47, which deals with the Sabbath controversy through the healing of a paralytic. Verses 1-3 describe the scene:

> *¹After these things there was a feast of the Jews; and Yeshua went up to Jerusalem. ²Now there is in Jerusalem by the sheep gate a pool, which is called in Hebrew Bethesda, having five porches. ³In these lay a multitude of them that were sick, blind, halt, withered.*

As in verse 1, generally, if *a* feast is mentioned but not specifically named, it would be the Feast of the Passover. If this is the case, then this is the second Passover mentioned in *Yeshua's* public ministry, which was about a year-and-a-half old. In verses 2-3, the Pool of Bethesda is introduced, a pool now located in the Muslim Quarter of the Old City that has been uncovered in recent times.

> *⁵And a certain man was there, who had been thirty and eight years in his infirmity. ⁶When Yeshua saw him lying, and knew that he had been now a long time in that case, he said unto him, Would you be made whole? ⁷The sick man answered him, Sir, I have no man, when the water is troubled, to put me into the pool: but while I am coming, another steps down before me. ⁸Yeshua said unto him, Arise, take up your bed, and walk. ⁹And straightway the man was made whole, and took up his bed and walked.*

In verse 5, *Yeshua* went to the Pool of Bethesda and saw a man lying there who had been ailing for thirty-eight years. In verse 6, He asked the man if he wanted to be healed and received a positive answer in verse 7. Then, in verse 8, the Messiah told him to do something that went contrary to the Jewish practice of that day: *Arise, take up your bed, and walk.* In verse 9a, the man was healed immediately. Important is the detail John mentioned in verse 9b:

Now it was the sabbath on that day.

What *Yeshua* had asked the man to do was a breach of the Pharisaic interpretation of keeping the Sabbath. Among the fifteen hundred Sabbath rules was one that forbade a person to carry a burden from a public place to a private place or from a private place to a public place. *Yeshua* knew that asking the man to pick up his bed would raise the issue regarding His messianic claims, but He wanted the people and the leaders, in particular, to come to a decision concerning Him.

After the man's physical healing at the Pool of Bethesda, he was quickly confronted in verse 10:

So the Jews said unto him that was cured, It is the sabbath, and it is not lawful for you to take up your bed.

The man was questioned further by the Pharisaic Jews in verses 11-13:

[11]But he answered them, He that made me whole, the same said unto me, Take up your bed, and walk. [12]They asked him, Who is the man that said unto you, Take up your bed, and walk? [13]But he that was healed knew not who it was; for Yeshua had conveyed himself away, a multitude being in the place.

The man's response in verse 11 was that the One who had healed him told him to do this. In verse 12, they asked him who it was that healed him. In verse 13, the former paralytic said he did not know. The spiritual healing of the man is recorded in verses 14-15:

¹⁴Afterward Yeshua finds him in the temple, and said unto him, Behold, you are made whole: sin no more, lest a worse thing befall you. ¹⁵The man went away, and told the Jews that it was Yeshua who had made him whole.

In verse 14, after the healing, *Yeshua* found the man again, this time in the Temple where he was perhaps thanking God for his healing and participating in the Temple festivities of the feast. He told the man, *Behold, you are made whole: sin no more, lest a worse thing befall you.* This indicates the spiritual healing of the man. At that point, he discovered who *Yeshua* was, and he informed the others in verse 15. There is no need to see anything sinister here. Although the response of the hearers was negative, the motive of the former paralytic may have been nothing more than to give them the information they were seeking.

This incident led to two specific accusations against *Yeshua* in verses 16-18. The first accusation came in verse 16:

And for this cause the Jews persecuted Yeshua, because he did these things on the sabbath.

The first accusation was that He had healed someone on the Sabbath day. This did not violate the Mosaic Law, but it did break Pharisaic law that forbade healing on the Sabbath day, except in one situation, if there was a danger to life. As long as the man's life was not endangered, he should not have been healed on this day. John stated that this was a key reason why they persecuted the Messiah. *Yeshua's* answer is given in verse 17:

But Yeshua answered them, My Father works even until now, and I work.

This answer brought on the second accusation in verse 18:

For this cause therefore the Jews sought the more to kill him, because he not only broke the sabbath, but also called God his own Father, making himself equal with God.

To a Jewish audience, calling God His own unique Father meant He was making Himself an equal with God. Cultic groups tend to deny the deity of the Son, often on the basis that a son is less than his father; therefore, if *Yeshua* is the Son of God, He must be less than God. This was not true in Jewish reckoning, because the firstborn son is considered to be equal to the father. The real issue is what did the Jewish audience understand Him to mean when they heard Him speak? When He stated: *My Father works..., and I work,* they clearly understood that He was claiming to be equal with God. There was no ambiguity in the Jewish mind about what He was claiming.

Yeshua defended Himself by making four specific points in verses 19-29. The first point of His defense is given in verses 19-21:

[19]Yeshua therefore answered and said unto them, Verily, verily, I say unto you, The Son can do nothing of himself, but what he sees the Father doing: for what things soever he does, these the Son also does in like manner. [20]For the Father loves the Son, and shows him all things that himself does: and greater works than these will he show him, that ye may marvel. [21]For as the Father raises the dead and gives them life, even so the Son also gives life to whom he will.

He was doing the works of the Father in three ways. First, in verse 19, He has an equal relationship with the Father; what One does, the other does. The works of the Father are also the works of the Son. If it is the work of the Son, it is also the work of the Father. Second, in verse 20, there is also equal love between the Father and the Son; both give rise to equally mighty works. Third, in verse 21, there is equal power; the Son shares the Father's power to give life. The giving of life was a divine ability; therefore, He must be divine. Because He does the works of the Father, works that only God can do, it means that He must be God.

The second point of *Yeshua's* defense was that the Son will judge all men, according to verse 22-23:

[22]For neither does the Father judge any man, but he has given all judgment unto the Son; [23]that all may honor the Son, even as they honor the Father. He that honors not the Son honors not the Father that sent him.

In the Old Testament, the final judgment is the prerogative of God. If the Son is the One who will do the judging, the Son must also be God. This also means the Son has equal honor with the Father.

The third point of His defense was that He has the power to provide eternal life, according to verse 24:

> Verily, verily, I say unto you, He that hears my word, and believes him that sent me, has eternal life, and comes not into judgment, but has passed out of death into life.

In the Old Testament, the One who has the ability to provide eternal life is God. Therefore, if the Son has the power to provide eternal life, He too must be God.

The fourth point of *Yeshua's* defense was that He will be the One to bring about the resurrection of the dead in verses 25-29:

> [25] *Verily, verily, I say unto you, The hour comes, and now is, when the dead shall hear the voice of the Son of God; and they that hear shall live.* [26] *For as the Father has life in himself, even so gave he to the Son also to have life in himself;* [27] *and he gave him authority to execute judgment, because he is a son of man.* [28] *Marvel not at this: for the hour comes, in which all that are in the tombs shall hear his voice,* [29] *and shall come forth; they that have done good, unto the resurrection of life; and they that have done evil, unto the resurrection of judgment.*

In the Old Testament, only God brought about the resurrection of the dead. If the Son is the One who will raise the dead, it means He must also be God. Therefore, *Yeshua* is the God-Man, and both facets are stated here in title form. In verse 25, He is the *Son of God*, emphasizing His deity; in verse 27, He is a *son of man*, emphasizing His humanity. Verse 29 points out that there will be two distinct kinds of resurrections. For the believer, it will be the *resurrection of life* or what the Book of Revelation calls the *first resurrection* (Rev. 20:5). For the unbeliever, it will be the *resurrection of judgment*, also known as the second resurrection, which leads to the second death (Rev. 21:8).

After He made these four claims to being the God-Man, *Yeshua* showed that there was a fourfold witness to His messianic claims.

> [30] *I can of myself do nothing: as I hear, I judge: and my judgment is righteous; because I seek not mine own will, but the will of him that sent me.* [31]*If I bear witness of myself, my witness is not true.* [32]*It is another that bears witness of me; and I know that the witness which he witnesses of me is true.*

In the Law of Moses, two or three witnesses were sufficient to establish a case. Why then did *Yeshua* provide four witnesses who support His claims? By doing so, He went beyond the demands of the Law.

The first witness was John the Baptist in verses 33-35:

> [33]*Ye have sent unto John, and he has borne witness unto the truth.* [34]*But the witness which I receive is not from man: howbeit I say these things, that ye may be saved.* [35]*He was the lamp that burns and shines; and ye were willing to rejoice for a season in his light.*

It was John who identified *Yeshua* as the *Lamb of God that takes away the sin of the world* (Jn. 1:29).

The second witness was that His works, His miracles, authenticated His claims in verse 36:

> *But the witness which I have is greater than that of John; for the works which the Father has given me to accomplish, the very works that I do, bear witness of me, that the Father has sent me.*

The third witness was God the Father in verses 37-38:

> [37]*And the Father that sent me, he has borne witness of me. Ye have neither heard his voice at any time, nor seen his form.* [38]*And ye have not his word abiding in you: for whom he sent, him ye believe not.*

God the Father spoke audibly at the Son's baptism when He declared out of Heaven: *This is my beloved Son in whom I am well pleased* (Mat. 3:13-17; Mk. 1:9-11; Lk. 3:21).

The fourth witness was the Scriptures in verses 39-47. The Scriptures bore witness because He was fulfilling the prophecies of His First Coming in verse 39:

Ye search the scriptures, because ye think that in them ye have eternal life; and these are they which bear witness of me; . . .

Because the Pharisees did not understand Scripture, they failed to understand Him in verses 40-44:

. . . [40]and ye will not come to me, that ye may have life. [41]I receive not glory from men. [42]But I know you, that ye have not the love of God in yourselves. [43]I am come in my Father's name, and ye receive me not: if another shall come in his own name, him ye will receive. [44]How can ye believe, who receive glory one of another, and the glory that comes from the only God ye seek not?

Because they did not understand Scripture, they did not have the love of God; they sought the glory of men, not the glory of God. Therefore, the very Law of Moses on which they had set their hope condemned them in verse 45:

Think not that I will accuse you to the Father: there is one that accuses you, even Moses, on whom ye have set your hope.

With four witnesses such as these, the problem was not that there was a lack of testimony to His messianic claims. *Yeshua* said that the real problem was their failure to believe Moses in verses 46-47:

[46]For if ye believed Moses, ye would believe me; for he wrote of me. [47]But if ye believe not his writings, how shall ye believe my words?

Accusing the Pharisees of not believing in Moses seems to be a stretch. It would be like approaching an ultra-Orthodox Jew today and saying, "You do not believe in the Mosaic Law." Who is more zealous for this Law? Yet it was a valid accusation. The Pharisees believed in Mosaic Law as it had been reinterpreted through the *Mishnah*. They did not believe Moses "as it was written." Had they accepted Mosaic Law as it was written, they would not have failed to recognize that He was the Messiah.

d. The Controversy over the Grain

The Sabbath controversy over the grain is mentioned in three of the Gospels. Verse 1 of Luke 6 provides the historical background to this controversy:

> *¹Now it came to pass on a sabbath, that he was going through the grainfields; and his disciples plucked the ears, and did eat, rubbing them in their hands. ²But certain of the Pharisees said, Why do ye that which it is not lawful to do on the sabbath day?*

Verse 2 records the Pharisees' attack, which occurred because the disciples had broken four of those fifteen hundred rules and regulations: When they took the wheat off the stalk, they were guilty of reaping. When they rubbed the wheat in their hands in order to separate it from the chaff, they were guilty of threshing. When they blew into their hands to blow the chaff away, they were guilty of winnowing. And lastly, when they swallowed the wheat, they were guilty of storing the wheat. This is how extreme the "building of the fence" had become by this time.

Because of these rules, some Pharisees would not walk on the grass on the Sabbath day. If someone asked such a rabbi, "What is wrong with walking on the grass on the Sabbath day," his answer would be, "Nothing. It is permissible to walk on the grass on the Sabbath day." However, there is a problem. What looks only like a grassy field might have one stalk of wheat growing wild in it. A person walking through the field of grass might inadvertently step on that one stalk of wheat, separate the wheat from its stalk, and become guilty of reaping on the Sabbath day. Furthermore, if his foot came down and twisted the wheat just enough to separate the wheat from the chaff, he would be guilty of threshing on the Sabbath day. If he continued to walk, the outer hem of his garment might create just enough breeze to blow the chaff away, and he would be guilty of winnowing on the Sabbath day. Finally, once the person had gone, a bird or rodent might see the exposed piece of wheat and swallow it, causing him to be guilty of storing the wheat on the Sabbath day.

Yeshua responded by making six statements. First, He made an historical appeal to King David in verses 3-4:

> ³*And Yeshua answering them said, Have ye not read even this, what David did, when he was hungry, he, and they that were with him;* ⁴*how he entered into the house of God, and took and ate the showbread, and gave also to them that were with him; which it is not lawful to eat save for the priests alone?*

He pointed out that David also violated Pharisaic law when he ate the *showbread*. Moses never said that a Levite could not give the *showbread* to a non-Levite. Pharisaic law, however, did say that. In the case of the Pharisees, they could not claim that David lived before the Oral Law, because in their theology, God gave the Oral Law to Moses; therefore, it preceded the time of David. So David himself broke Pharisaic law, yet they never condemned David. If David could break Pharisaic law, so could David's greater Son (Mat. 12:3-4; Mk. 2:25-26).

Second, the Law of Sabbath Rest did not apply in every situation, according to Matthew 12:5:

> *Or have ye not read in the law, that on the sabbath day the priests in the temple profane the sabbath, and are guiltless?*

One such situation was the Temple Compound. For those in the Temple Compound, it was not a day of rest, but a day of labor. In fact, those in the compound had to work harder on the Sabbath day than a normal day. There were daily sacrifices and rituals, but on the Sabbath, all sacrifices were doubled. Furthermore, there were special rituals performed only on the Sabbath. Therefore, the Sabbath was not a day of rest for those working within the Temple Compound. This shows that the Law of Moses allowed and even commanded certain works to be done on the Sabbath day. Even the Pharisees allowed certain works such as midwifery, circumcision, and the preparation of a corpse on the Sabbath day. The point was that the Law of Sabbath Rest did not apply to every specific situation.

Third, as the Messiah, He is greater than the Temple, according to Matthew 12:6:

> *But I say unto you, that one greater than the temple is here.*

If the Temple allowed certain works to be done on the Sabbath without violating the Law of Sabbath Rest, so could He allow certain works without breaking that law.

Fourth, He pointed out that certain works were always allowed on the Sabbath day as stated in Matthew 12:7:

> *But if ye had known what this means, I desire mercy, and not sacrifice, ye would not have condemned the guiltless.*

Quoting Hosea 6:6, works of necessity such as eating and works of mercy such as healing were always allowed on the Sabbath day.

Fifth, as the Messiah, He was the Lord of the Sabbath in Luke 6:5:

> *And he said unto them, The Son of man is lord of the sabbath.*

As Lord of the Sabbath, He could allow what they disallowed, and He could disallow what they allowed. As long as He did not violate the Mosaic Law, they had no grounds for any accusation against Him (Mat. 12:8; Mk. 2:28).

And sixth, He declared that they had totally misconstrued the purpose of the Sabbath in Mark 2:27:

> *And he said unto them, The sabbath was made for man, and not man for the sabbath: . . .*

Pharisaic Judaism taught that the reason God made Israel was for honoring the Sabbath. Therefore, Israel was made for the Sabbath. *Yeshua*, however, taught that the exact opposite was true. Israel was not made for the Sabbath; the Sabbath was made for Israel. The purpose of the Sabbath was to give Israel a day of refreshment and rest, not to enslave Israel to Sabbath laws. Yet these fifteen hundred additional rules and regulations had the effect of enslaving Jews to the Sabbath. Therefore, they had totally misconstrued the purpose of the Sabbath.

e. The Healing of the Man with the Withered Hand

The fifth Sabbath event in the Gospels is the controversy concerning the healing of the man with the withered hand. Three of the Gospels record this event: Matthew 12:9-14, Mark 3:1-6, and Luke 6:6-11. This particular controversy took place in the synagogue. According to Luke's account, *Yeshua* was expounding the Word. In Luke 6:6 we read:

> *And it came to pass on another sabbath, that he entered into the synagogue and taught: and there was a man there, and his right hand was withered.*

On that Sabbath, there was a man in the audience who happened to have a withered hand. This was a medical problem, but it was not life threatening. Again, Luke's profession becomes evident. Both Matthew's account and Mark's account simply state that the man's hand was withered; however, Doctor Luke specifies it was his *right hand*. Verse 7 states:

> *And the scribes and the Pharisees watched him, whether he would heal on the sabbath; that they might find how to accuse him.*

It appears that the man was a plant for the purpose of entrapment, because Matthew 12:10 states that members of the audience asked:

> *Is it lawful to heal on the sabbath day? with the goal that they might accuse him.*

Yeshua clearly understood what the circumstances were in Luke 6:8:

> *But he knew their thoughts; and he said to the man that had his hand withered, Rise up, and stand forth in the midst. And he arose and stood forth.*

Nevertheless, He again showed that He would not accept their Pharisaic Mishnaic authority. He began by reminding them of their own particular practice in Matthew 12:11-12:

[11] And he said unto them, What man shall there be of you, that shall have one sheep, and if this fall into a pit on the sabbath day, will he not lay hold on it, and lift it out? [12] How much then is a man of more value than a sheep! Wherefore it is lawful to do good on the sabbath day.

This shows that even they believed that it was permitted to do good on the Sabbath. However, He challenged them with a question in Luke 6:9:

And Yeshua said unto them, I ask you, Is it lawful on the sabbath to do good, or to do harm? to save a life, or to destroy it?

According to Mark 3:4, they chose to remain silent. He used a type of argument called *kal v'chomer*, which argues from the lesser to the greater. He stated that if it was permissible to do good for an animal on the Sabbath day, the lesser, how much more would it be permissible to do good for a man on the Sabbath day, the greater? He repeated two lessons previously mentioned: First, works of necessity and works of mercy were allowed on the Sabbath day, even for animals. Second, healing was an act of mercy; therefore, it did not violate the Sabbath. Having made His point, He proceeded to heal the man's hand in Luke 6:10:

And he looked round about on them all, and said unto him, Stretch forth your hand. And he did so: and his hand was restored.

By doing so, He again showed His negation of Pharisaic authority. The wording of Mark 3:5 implies that He did it to spite them. The means of healing was merely by ordering the man to stretch out his right hand, and he was immediately healed. *Yeshua* did not ask the man if he believed or had faith; at that point, faith was not essential. Although the man himself was a plant, *Yeshua* went ahead and healed him, because at this point in His career, the purpose of His miracles was to authenticate His messianic claims.

The Pharisaic response to this incident and to the Sabbath controversies in general is given in Luke 6:11:

> *But they were filled with madness; and communed one with another what they might do to Yeshua.*

Their response was threefold. First, in verse 11 *they were filled with madness.* They let the emotion of anger control them. They could no longer think logically and rationally.

Second, according to Matthew 12:14:

> *But the Pharisees went out, and took counsel against him, how they might destroy him.*

They conspired how to be rid of Him in one form or another and how to reject His messianic claims, in spite of His special abilities.

Third, according to Mark 3:6:

> *And the Pharisees went out, and straightway with the Herodians took counsel against him, how they might destroy him.*

The Pharisees joined with the Herodians in their conspiracy against *Yeshua.* This, indeed, made for strange bedfellows, because they were at the opposite ends of the political spectrum and bitter enemies toward each other. The Pharisees were opposed to Roman rule in any form, but the Herodians were willing to accept Roman rule if it came through the House of Herod. Yet, on the issue of *Yeshua,* they had a common cause.

f. The Second Visit to Nazareth

The sixth Sabbath event was the second visit to Nazareth. This is recorded in two of the Gospels: Matthew 13:54-58 and Mark 6:1-6. Basically, the two passages together indicate that Yeshua taught in the synagogue in which He had grown up, but for the second time, He was rejected insofar as His messianic claims were concerned.

g. Sabbath Healing and the Keeping of the Law

The seventh Sabbath event was the healing on the Sabbath and the keeping of the Law, recorded only by one Gospel writer, John. In John 7:21-24, four things emerge.

> *²¹ Yeshua answered and said unto them, I did one work, and you all marvel because thereof. ²² Moses has given you circumcision (not that it is of Moses, but of the fathers); and on the sabbath you circumcise a man. ²³ If a man receives circumcision on the sabbath, that the law of Moses may not be broken; are you wroth with me, because I made a man every whit whole on the sabbath? ²⁴ Judge not according to appearance, but judge righteous judgment.*

In verse 21, the problem of the Messiah's accusers was their misinterpretation as to the meaning of the Sabbath. The reason they believed He broke the Sabbath by healing on the Sabbath was because of their misinterpretation of the Sabbath.

Circumcision was part of the Law of Moses; even they performed circumcision on the Sabbath day according to verse 22.

In verse 23, if circumcision is allowed on the Sabbath, so healing is allowed on the Sabbath day.

Yeshua made the application in verse 24: Therefore, *judge righteous judgment*. If it is permissible to mutilate on the Sabbath—and circumcision is a form of mutilation—it is permissible to heal on the Sabbath day. Furthermore, Sabbath rest included being healed on the Sabbath day.

h. The Healing of a Man Born Blind

The eighth Sabbath event is the controversy over the healing of the man born blind, recorded in only one Gospel, John 9:1-41. There are five subdivisions in this passage.

First, the physical healing of the man born blind is in verses 1-12. *Yeshua* healed a man who was born blind, and by so doing He violated the Sabbath according to Pharisaism.

The second subdivision, verses 13-17, is the first interrogation of the man born blind. Because it was a Sabbath when *Yeshua* opened his eyes, He violated the Sabbath in verse 14. Furthermore, *Yeshua* healed the man in a way forbidden by Pharisaic law: "Wine cannot be injected into the eye, but may be put on the eye lids. Spittle is forbidden even on the eyelids." One was forbidden to heal in this very way on the Sabbath day. The conclusion of the rabbis was that *Yeshua* could not be from God because He did not keep the Sabbath: He healed on the Sabbath. However, they could not deny the uniqueness of this miracle, so they hoped to find a loophole and proposed that maybe the man really was not born blind.

In the third subdivision, verses 18-22, they interrogated the parents. The parents affirmed that this man was their son and that he was born blind.

In the fourth subdivision, verses 23-34, they interrogated the man born blind for the second time. They tried to convince him that *Yeshua* was a false teacher, but the man refused to be convinced.

And in the fifth subdivision, verses 35-41, the spiritual healing of the man came when he accepted *Yeshua* as the Son of God.

i. The Healing of the Crippled Woman

The ninth Sabbath event is the controversy over the healing of the crippled woman, again found only in one Gospel, Luke 13:10-17.

> *[10] And he was teaching in one of the synagogues on the sabbath day. [11] And behold, a woman that had a spirit of infirmity eighteen years; and she was bowed together, and could in no wise lift herself up. [12] And when Yeshua saw her, he called her, and said to her, Woman, you are loosed from your infirmity. [13] And he laid his hands upon her: and immediately she was made straight, and glorified God. [14] And the ruler of the synagogue, being moved with indignation because Yeshua had healed on the sabbath, answered and said to the multitude, There are six days in which men ought to work: in them therefore come and be healed, and not on the day of the sabbath. [15] But the Lord answered him, and said, You hypocrites, does not each one of you on the sabbath loose*

> *his ox or his ass from the stall, and lead him away to watering?* ¹⁶ *And ought not this woman, being a daughter of Abraham, whom Satan had bound, lo, these eighteen years, to have been loosed from this bond on the day of the sabbath?* ¹⁷ *And as he said these things, all his adversaries were put to shame: and all the multitude rejoiced for all the glorious things that were done by him.*

In verse 10, *Yeshua* was teaching in the synagogue on the Sabbath day. Verse 11 states that there was a woman in the service who had curvature of the spine; she had had this condition now for eighteen years. In verses 12-13, *Yeshua* proceeded to heal her curvature of the spine.

In verse 14, this brought a negative reaction from the ruler or president of the synagogue. He was moved with indignation because *Yeshua* healed on the Sabbath and then said: *There are six days in which men ought to work: in them therefore come and be healed, and not on the day of the sabbath.*

But in verse 15, *Yeshua* reminded them that even the Pharisees would release their ox or their donkey from the stall and lead them to water on the Sabbath day. In verse 16, even more so should this woman have been released from her bondage on the Sabbath day. In verse 17, the result was that the critics were silenced while *all the multitude rejoiced.* The point of the passage, again, is that Sabbath rest included being healed on the Sabbath day.

j. The Healing of the Man with Dropsy

The tenth Sabbath event is the controversy dealing with the healing of the man with dropsy, also recorded only by one Gospel writer, Luke 14:1-6.

> ¹ *And it came to pass, when he went into the house of one of the rulers of the Pharisees on a sabbath to eat bread, that they were watching him.* ² *And behold, there was before him a certain man that had the dropsy.* ³ *And Yeshua answering spoke unto the lawyers and Pharisees, saying, Is it lawful to heal on the sabbath, or not?* ⁴ *But they held their peace. And he took him, and healed him, and let him go.* ⁵ *And he said unto them, Which of you shall have an ass or an ox fallen into*

> *a well, and will not straightway draw him up on a sabbath day?* [6] *And they could not answer again unto these things.*

In verse 1, *Yeshua* was dining in the home of a Pharisee on a Sabbath. Included among the guests was the man who had the dropsy. In verse 3, *Yeshua* asked them whether or not it is lawful to heal on the Sabbath. In verse 4, they chose to remain silent and *Yeshua* healed the man on the Sabbath. In verse 5, He reminded them that they themselves believed that if an ox or a donkey fell into a pit on the Sabbath day, it was permissible to rescue the animal. If it was permissible to rescue an animal, it was more permissible to rescue a man on the Sabbath day. Verse 6 points out that they were unable to respond to His argument.

There are two observations in this passage. First, if it is permissible to do good to animals on the Sabbath, it is even more permissible to do good to man. And second, Sabbath rest included being healed.

k. The Sabbath in the Great Tribulation

The eleventh Sabbath event had to do with the Sabbath in the Great Tribulation, recorded by one Gospel writer, Matthew 24:20:

> *And pray ye that your flight be not in the winter, neither on a sabbath: . . .*

Israel will flee the Land in the middle of the Tribulation. Due to rabbinic limitations on traveling on the Sabbath day, the success of the escape will be hindered if the event falls on the Sabbath day.

l. The Sabbath and the Death and Burial of the Messiah

The twelfth Sabbath event is the death and burial of the Messiah. This is mentioned in four passages by three Gospel writers: once by Mark, twice by Luke, and once by John.

The first passage is Mark 15:42:

> *And when even was now come, because it was the Preparation, that is, the day before the sabbath, . . .*

The second passage is Luke 23:54:

And it was the day of the Preparation [Friday], *and the sabbath drew on* [sundown Friday].

The third passage is Luke 23:56:

And on the sabbath they rested according to the commandment [of Moses].

And the fourth passage is John 19:31:

The Jews therefore, because it was the Preparation [Friday], *that the bodies should not remain on the cross upon the sabbath* [after sundown Friday], *(for the day of that sabbath was a high day),* . . .

That Sabbath day was also the first day of the Feast of Unleavened Bread, making it a High Sabbath.

Five observations in these passages should be noted. First, these are all references to Friday preceding the start of the Sabbath at sundown. Second, they show that *Yeshua* did die on a Friday. Third, *the day of Preparation* always means "in preparation for the Sabbath," which was the day before the Sabbath; as the Sabbath draws nigh, it is still Friday. Fourth, *Yeshua* was placed in the tomb on Friday. And fifth, He was in the tomb throughout the Sabbath, through sundown Saturday.

m. The Sabbath Visit to the Tomb

The thirteenth and final Sabbath event is the visit of the women to the tomb, mentioned in two of the Gospels. The first passage is Matthew 28:1:

Now late on the sabbath day, as it began to dawn toward the first day of the week, came Mary Magdalene and the other Mary to see the sepulcher.

In Gentile reckoning, this sounds like the wee hours of Sunday morning. Actually, it is nearing sundown Saturday evening.

The second passage is Mark 16:1:

And when the sabbath was past, Mary Magdalene, and Mary the mother of James, and Salome, brought spices, that they might come and anoint him.

In Jewish reckoning, the passing of the Sabbath and the dawn of the first day of the week are always Saturday evening. On Saturday evening, as it was moving toward Saturday night, the women came to visit the tomb for the purpose of anointing the body.

2. Observations and Conclusions

Four observations and conclusions can be made concerning the thirteen Sabbath events in the Gospels: the areas of conflict, the Sabbath in Rabbinic Judaism, *Yeshua's* interpretation of the Sabbath, and no mandate for Sabbath-keeping.

a. The Areas of Conflict

There were three major areas of conflict between *Yeshua* and the Pharisees. The first area of conflict had to do with His claim to be the Messiah. A second major area of conflict had to do with the authority of the *Mishnah*, the authority of rabbinic tradition over such things as fasting and eating with unwashed hands. And the third area of conflict between *Yeshua* and the Pharisees had to do with the proper way of observing the Sabbath.

b. The Sabbath in Rabbinic Judaism

By this time, the Sabbath had become the second most important element in Rabbinic Judaism. People firmly believed that Israel was created for the purpose of observing the Sabbath. The rabbis had passed one thousand five hundred additional Sabbath rules and regulations, far beyond what the Law of Moses commanded. By passing these additional Sabbath regulations, they made Sabbath rest a burden. The Sabbath had become personified as a bride, a princess, and a queen.

c. Yeshua's Interpretation of the Sabbath

Yeshua accused the Pharisees of totally misconstruing the purpose of the Sabbath, which was to help man, not to enslave him. The Sabbath was made for man, not man for the Sabbath (Mk. 2:27), or, to put it in rabbinic terms, the Sabbath was made for Israel, not that Israel was made for the Sabbath. He consistently emphasized the human element in the purpose of the Sabbath.

Yeshua claimed to be the *lord of the sabbath* (Mat. 12:8). As Lord of the Sabbath, He could permit what the Pharisees had forbidden on the Sabbath, but He could also forbid what they permitted on the Sabbath.

Yeshua Himself was scrupulous in observing the Sabbath. However, He did not observe the Sabbath in the manner prescribed by the rabbis or the Pharisees; He observed it in the manner prescribed by the Law of Moses. He followed certain traditions of the rabbis, such as going to synagogue on the Sabbath, but this was not something He made mandatory. However, this fact is not evidence that the Sabbath is mandatory today. Both Jewish and Gentile believers often make the Sabbath mandatory based on the fact that *Yeshua* kept the Sabbath. Yes, He kept the Sabbath according to the Law of Moses, but this is not evidence that the Sabbath is mandatory today. Remember, *Yeshua* lived under the Law of Moses and had to obey the commandments of the Law of Moses, not only the Sabbath commandment, but all 613 commandments which were applicable to Him, regardless of what category they were in, whether they were moral commandments, civil commandments, ceremonial commandments, or whatever. To insist on keeping the Sabbath because *Yeshua* kept the Sabbath would also require us to keep all the other commandments down to every jot and tittle. This would include those that are categorized as civil commandments and ceremonial commandments.

Of the many, many commandments that *Yeshua* Himself issued in the course of His ministry—such as those which are found in His Upper Room Discourse—the Sabbath is never one of them. This is where Sabbath-keepers have a problem. They do not find a single command *Yeshua* issued to keep the Sabbath. *Yeshua* issued many commandments, including commandments which are also found in the Law of Moses; however, the Sabbath commandment was never one of them.

d. No Mandate for Sabbath-Keeping

The fourth observation and conclusion is that nothing in any of these thirteen Sabbath events in the Gospels shows that Sabbath-keeping is mandatory for believers today. The keeping of the Sabbath, insofar as the

Gospels are concerned, is not the rule of life for the New Testament believer.

B. The Sabbath in the Book of Acts

In the second section of the study of the Sabbath in the New Testament, we will be looking at the Book of Acts. In it, the Sabbath is mentioned a total of nine times.

1. The Sabbath Passages

The first time the word appears in the Book of Acts is in 1:12, where it is simply mentioned as a measure of distance: *a sabbath day's journey*. A Sabbath day's journey was the distance between Jerusalem and the Mount of Olives. The rabbis came up with the Sabbath day's journey based upon Joshua 3:4. It was *two thousand cubits* or 2,000 paces or 3,000 feet, approximately the distance of three-quarters of a mile or a modern day kilometer.

The other eight times that the Sabbath is mentioned in the Book of Acts are always in conjunction with the service in the synagogue: Acts 13:14, the synagogue service in Antioch of Pisidia; Acts 13:27, the synagogue service in Jerusalem; Acts 13:42, the synagogue service in Antioch of Pisidia; Acts 13:44, again the synagogue service in Antioch of Pisidia; Acts 15:21, the synagogue Sabbath services in all cities; Acts 16:13, a synagogue service by the riverside in the town of Philippi; Acts 17:2, the synagogue service in Thessalonica; and Acts 18:4, the synagogue service in Corinth.

2. Observations

There are six observations to be noted from these passages. First, every reference to the Sabbath, except for the passage in Acts 1:12, deals with the synagogue service. There is not a single Sabbath reference in connection with the worship service of believers.

Second, these were all gatherings of unbelievers, not believers.

Third, Paul went to the synagogue on the Sabbath day, but it was not for the purpose of corporate worship with believers, it was for the purpose of evangelism.

Fourth, those saved in the synagogue because of Paul's preaching, eventually left the synagogue and became part of the local congregation of believers.

Fifth, there is no single record in the Book of Acts that the believers met on the Sabbath day.

Sixth, there is no Sabbath commandment for either the individual or for the local congregation concerning the Sabbath.

The obvious conclusion is that there is no basis for mandatory Sabbath-keeping in the Book of Acts.

3. Jewish Believers in the Synagogue

The point is sometimes made that Jewish believers continued going to synagogue on the Sabbath day. This would seem to show that they felt it was obligatory to observe the Sabbath. It is true that Jewish believers did continue to attend the synagogue as late as A.D. 90. This was the year when the special benediction was issued at the Sabbath service that essentially forced Jewish believers out of the synagogue.

However, this does not prove anything. Again, there is no command in the Book of Acts to hold corporate worship on the Sabbath. The presence of Jewish believers in the synagogue did not constitute the meeting of the local congregation. Some Jewish believers now and then still attend synagogue. They attend it on the Sabbath, but this is not the meeting of believers on the Sabbath day.

There was a variety of reasons why Jewish believers continued attending the synagogue or the Temple. One reason is that this was habit for some. Also there was social pressure upon Jewish believers to attend synagogue. Some, no doubt, were fearful of possible sanctions. In the case of Paul, this was part of his missionary policy; he went to synagogue on the Sabbath day to proclaim the gospel. We know from the Epistle of James that the Jerusalem Church had a very strong, conservative leadership, and this may be another reason they continued to attend the synagogue service. Finally, no doubt some had theological convictions that they still had to continue going to synagogue or to the Temple on the Sabbath day.

However, three basic facts should be noted. First, there is no command in the Book of Acts to meet on the Sabbath day. Second, there is no command to keep the Sabbath either individually or corporately as a day of rest or as a day of worship in the Book of Acts. And third, the Book of Acts provides not a single example for any congregation, Jewish or Gentile, to hold their meetings on the Sabbath day. Those who wish to use the actions of Jewish believers in the Book of Acts as a mandate should be consistent: They should go to synagogue services on the Sabbath, but this is not the meeting of believers.

4. Two Relevant Passages

There are two passages in the Book of Acts that, by themselves, do not deal with the Sabbath issue, but are somewhat relevant to it.

a. Acts 15:1-20

This passage deals with the Jerusalem Council. The actual issue before this council was that of Gentile circumcision in verse 1. Later, in verse 5 though, it was expanded to keeping the whole Law of Moses, so obviously, this would have included the Sabbath issue. Another important fact to note is that this passage deals primarily with what Gentile believers should or should not do rather than what Jewish believers should or should not do. The statement that becomes relevant to the Sabbath is found in verse 10:

> *Now therefore why make ye trial of God, that ye should put a yoke upon the neck of the disciples which neither our fathers nor we were able to bear?*

Four things are noteworthy about this verse: First, the *yoke* in this context is clearly the Law of Moses; second, if the Jews—the meaning of the phrase, *neither our fathers nor we*—were unable to keep the Law, there is no reason to ask the Gentiles to do what even Jewish believers could not do; third, neither circumcision nor Sabbath-keeping was made mandatory for Gentiles; and fourth, Peter's statement implies that these things were not obligatory upon Jews either, so Jewish believers were equally exempt from the Law of Moses.

Nowhere in Acts 15 is there a requirement to keep the Sabbath. If the Gentiles were obligated to keep the Sabbath, this would have been the place for the apostles to note it. But the Sabbath was not included among the list of the things they asked the Gentiles to observe.

b. Acts 21:20-24

The second relevant passage concerns Paul's meeting with the elders of the Jerusalem Church.

> [20] *And they, when they heard it, glorified God; and they said unto him, You see, brother, how many thousands there are among the Jews of them that have believed; and they are all zealous for the law:* [21] *and they have been informed concerning you, that you teach all the Jews who are among the Gentiles to forsake Moses, telling them not to circumcise their children neither to walk after the customs.* [22] *What is it therefore? they will certainly hear that you have come.* [23] *Do therefore this that we say to you: We have four men that have a vow on them;* [24] *these take, and purify yourself with them, and be at charges for them, that they may shave their heads: and all shall know that there is no truth in the things whereof they have been informed concerning thee; but that you yourself also walk orderly, keeping the law.*

This passage also contains four key truths. First, there is no specific mention of the Sabbath, but the Sabbath was part of the *law* of verse 20 and the *customs* of verse 21.

Second, this passage, however, only describes what Jewish believers in Jerusalem practiced and says nothing about mandatory Sabbath-keeping.

Third, to extrapolate mandatory Sabbath-keeping from this passage is to extrapolate too much. The Sabbath is not the only thing in the Law of Moses. The zealousness of the Jewish believers in Jerusalem included many other parts of the Law, including civil and ceremonial elements.

Fourth, all this passage teaches is that Jewish believers are free to keep the Law, including the freedom to observe the Sabbath, but not that they are required to do so.

5. Conclusion

There is no support for mandatory Sabbath-keeping for either Jews or Gentiles in the Book of Acts.

C. The Sabbath in the Epistles of Paul

Paul makes reference to the Sabbath only three times in his epistles, and only in the first passage is the word actually used.

1. The Passages

a. Colossians 2:16-17

¹⁶Let no man therefore judge you in meat, or in drink, or in respect of a feast day or a new moon or a sabbath day: ¹⁷which are a shadow of the things to come; but the body is Christ's.

This follows the context of verses 13-15, where Paul points out that the *ordinances,* which were against us, have been blotted out by the death of the Messiah. It is for that reason that there is no longer any obligation to keep the Law or any of its facets. He mentions several of these facets: first, *in meat or in drink,* which are the *kosher* laws, the laws of *kashrut,* the dietary laws; second, *a feast day,* such as Passover, Weeks, or Tabernacles; third, he mentions the *new moon,* the New Moon Festival; fourth, *a sabbath day.* Based upon these truths, Paul writes that, for that reason, one believer cannot judge another believer in these areas. These areas include the issue of the Sabbath. All of these, including the Sabbath, are only *a shadow of the things to come.*

In Hebrews 8:5, the writer pointed out that the entire Tabernacle system was a *shadow.* Because it was *a shadow,* it was no longer obligatory. In Hebrews 10:1, the Law, especially the sacrificial system, was *a shadow.* Because it was *a shadow,* it was no longer obligatory. With the Colossians passage, the same thing is true of the Sabbath: It was only *a shadow.* Because it was *a shadow,* it is no longer obligatory. If the Sabbath were still mandatory, failure to keep it would put the violator under divine judgment. This is exactly what the context states is no longer true.

D. R. de Lacey, in his chapter on "The Sabbath/Sunday Question and the Law in the Pauline Corpus," states:

> As with the law, the Sabbath has lost its intrinsic value, but may yet be enjoyed by those who wish to keep them...no stringent regulations are to be laid down over the use of Sabbath. As with the law, the believer is no longer bound by external stipulation as in the matter of festivals.[11]

The point of this Colossians context is that the ordinances, which were against us, have been blotted out by the death of the Messiah. Therefore, if we do not keep the Sabbath, we are not under divine judgment. "As with the law," de Lacey writes, "the Sabbath has lost its intrinsic value." Although they may yet be kept "by those who wish to keep them," neither the Law nor the Sabbath are "stringent regulations" for us to keep. The believer is not bound to the Sabbath, but is free from it.

b. Romans 14:4-6a

[4]Who are you that judges the servant of another? to his own lord he stands or falls. Yea, he shall be made to stand; for the Lord has power to make him stand. [5]One man esteems one day above another: another esteems every day alike. Let each man be fully assured in his own mind. [6]He that regards the day, regards it unto the Lord: ...

Verse 4 gives a clear prohibition against fellow believers judging one another concerning practice in various areas. One of these areas concerns the esteeming of days. While the term *day* is not limited to the Sabbath day, it would certainly be included. In verse 5, one man is free to esteem a day as being more important than another day, whether it is Saturday or Sunday. Another believer may view all days alike. Both are valid options according to this passage. In verse 6a, both options are to be taken as honoring the Lord.

---

[11] D. R. de Lacey, "The Sabbath/Sunday Question and the Law in the Pauline Corpus," in *From Sabbath to Lord's Day: A Biblical, Historical and Theological Investigation* (ed. D. A. Carson; Grand Rapids: Zondervan, 1982), 183.

The application for this passage includes three things: First, believers who choose not to keep the Sabbath should not judge those who keep it as legalists; second, those who do choose to keep the Sabbath are not to make their choice mandatory upon all other believers; and third, this passage is against mandatory Sabbath-keeping for either Jews or Gentiles.

c. Galatians 4:10

Ye observe days, and months, and seasons, and years.

The *days* include the Sabbath days. The *months* would be the New Moon Festivals. The *seasons* are the seven Holy Seasons of Leviticus 23. The *years* are the Sabbatical Years and the Year of Jubilee. The context of this Galatians passage is clearly the Law of Moses as a whole. This comes out in almost every chapter of the Book of Galatians except chapter 1 (2:16, 19-20; 3:2, 5, 10-29; 4:4-5, 21; 5:3-4, 14; 6:13). It is very obvious that the context of the Book of Galatians is the Law of Moses.

Paul plays down the value of *days, and months, and seasons, and years* in two areas: first, as a means of salvation; but second, also as a rule of life. Paul viewed any attempt to impose Sabbath-keeping upon the Gentiles as wrong. Any tendency by Gentile believers to submit themselves to the Law of Moses and to things such as the Sabbath is viewed as taking a step backward in the spiritual life, not a step forward.

2. Conclusion

These are the only passages where the Sabbath is mentioned in the epistles of Paul. The conclusion is simple. In not a single one of Paul's letters does he ever state that the Sabbath is mandatory for either Jews or Gentiles. One would think that if Sabbath-keeping were mandatory, he would have mentioned it at least once. However, in none of his letters does Paul mention the Sabbath as mandatory either for Jews or Gentiles.

After extensively evaluating Paul's writings, de Lacey concludes:

> What does this tell us about Paul's attitude to the Sabbath? The clear implication is that he refuses to dogmatize one way or the other. An individual may keep the Sabbath or not; presumably, in general Paul might have assumed that a Jewish

Christian would do so and a Gentile convert would not. The important factor was not which practice one adopted, but one's motives: to convert for inadequate reasons is reprehensible. Thus Paul was probably content to allow a wide variety of practice in the churches.[12]

D. The Sabbath in the Book of Hebrews

This section on the Sabbath in the New Testament will be dealt with in two parts: first, the two passages; and second, the typology of the Sabbath.

1. The Two Passages

The Book of Hebrews gives the messianic implications concerning the Sabbath in two passages. Both passages are found only in chapter 4 and are found within a specific context. The context in its entirety is Hebrews 3:7-4:13. Verses 4:3-4 state:

³For we who have believed do enter into that rest; even as he has said,
As I swore in my wrath,
They shall not enter into my rest:
although the works were finished from the foundation of the world. ⁴For he has said somewhere of the seventh day on this wise, And God rested on the seventh day from all his works; ...

The passage teaches salvation rest on the basis of Genesis 2:2-3, which deals with God's creation rest.

The second passage, Hebrews 4:9, is based on the Sabbath in the Mosaic Law:

There remains therefore a sabbath rest for the people of God.

---

[12] D. R. de Lacey, "The Sabbath/Sunday Question and the Law in the Pauline Corpus," in *From Sabbath to Lord's Day: A Biblical, Historical and Theological Investigation* (ed. D. A. Carson; Grand Rapids: Zondervan, 1982), 183-84.

In the context of these passages, the writer deals with the Sabbath in three ways: first, the Sabbath rest in the Old Testament; second, the present salvation rest; and third, the future Kingdom rest.

2. The Typology of the Sabbath

Five specific things should be noted concerning the messianic implications of the Sabbath given in the Book of Hebrews. First, the Book of Hebrews treats the Sabbath typologically rather than literally as a day of rest or a day of worship.

Second, the Old Testament background to this typological use of the Sabbath is found in Deuteronomy 12:9:

> ...for ye are not as yet come to the rest and to the inheritance, which Jehovah your God gives you.

The concept of rest was closely associated with the Sabbath, but in this passage, it was also associated with the Land of Israel.

The third point is that there is a background to the typological use of the Sabbath day in three Gospel passages. The first one is Matthew 11:28-30, which speaks of spiritual rest. The statement concerning spiritual rest in this passage immediately precedes the two Sabbath conflicts with the Pharisees over the proper way of observing the Sabbath (Mat. 12:1-14). The second Gospel background is Luke 4:16-21, where *Yeshua* used the Sabbath day to proclaim His Messiahship in Nazareth and therefore proclaimed salvation rest. The third Gospel passage is John 5:30, where in the context of the Sabbath, *Yeshua* offered Kingdom rest.

The fourth thing is that a short exposition of the Book of Hebrews passages will bring out the following points. Again, the context of Hebrews 3:7-4:13 treats the Sabbath and the concept of rest from the Old Testament typologically to emphasize two things: first, present salvation rest, and second, future Kingdom rest. The specific passage of Hebrews 4:3-4 teaches salvation rest on the basis of Genesis 2:2-3, which deals with God's creation rest. God's creation rest is interpreted typologically as referring to the present salvation rest. The second passage is Hebrews 4:9, which is based upon the Sabbath in the Law of Moses. This, too, is interpreted typologically of the future Kingdom rest.

And the fifth point is that there are two conclusions. First, the Epistle of Hebrews was written specifically to Jewish believers. If there is any epistle that should have mentioned the Sabbath as being mandatory for these Jewish believers, if not Gentile believers, it would have been the Epistle of Hebrews. This epistle says nothing about mandatory Sabbath-keeping. The second conclusion is that this very same thing is true of all the other Messianic Jewish Epistles written specifically to Jewish believers: James, I Peter, II Peter, and Jude. If the Sabbath were mandatory, it would have been mentioned in one of these five Messianic Jewish Epistles. Yet, not a single letter, which was written to Jewish believers, mentions mandatory Sabbath-keeping.

E. Summary and Conclusions

The day of the Sabbath was never changed from Saturday to Sunday. Nowhere in the New Testament is Sunday called "the new Sabbath." Although the Sabbath is still from sundown Friday until sundown Saturday, there is no obligation any longer to observe it.

The Jewish believer is free from the Law of Moses and from mandatory Sabbath-keeping. He is still free to observe the Sabbath if he so chooses and in whatever manner he may choose. Any believer, Jewish or Gentile, is free to observe the Sabbath, whether it is as a day of rest or as a day of corporate worship or both. The day of choice is purely optional. A day does not even need to be chosen, as Paul so clearly brought out.

How this applies to the individual is seen in two ways: First, each believer, Jew or Gentile, has the option to set a day aside or not to set it aside; second, if he does choose to set a day aside however, he is free to choose any day of the week, Saturday, Sunday, or Thursday, or whatever.

How this applies corporately is also seen in two ways. First, the church or congregation must meet. The clear obligation in Hebrews 10:25 is that there must be the gathering of believers under elders and deacons. Second, the day of the week is up to the individual local congregation. Most churches have chosen Sunday; that is fine. Many messianic congregations have chosen Saturday; that is fine. In Muslim countries, churches have chosen Friday; that is fine. Any day of the week that the individual assembly wishes to choose, it is free to do so.

VIII. THE ISSUE OF SUNDAY

This chapter in the study of the Sabbath deals with the issue of Sunday. Covenant Theologians often insist that Sunday is now what the Sabbath used to be and that the Sabbath laws apply to it. The questions arise where this misconception originated and how it can be resolved.

A. The Origin of Sunday Observance

1. The Misconception

There is a current misconception being propagated, especially in certain Seventh Day Adventists circles, that the Sunday service began with Catholicism. Often they will try to say that the Sunday service originated with a law and a church council. The law cited is the Law of Constantine in A.D. 321, which declared that Sunday was the proper day of observance. There was also the Council of Laodicea in A.D. 364, which decreed that Sunday was the proper time to have the service. Thus, they claim that Sunday observance began with Catholicism.

However, historical reality is otherwise. Historically, Sunday worship became the universal practice of all churches outside the Land of Israel by the beginning of the second century. History will bear this out. The church councils did not initiate Sunday worship. What the church councils did was merely ratify a practice that was already quite common. The origin of the Sunday service was not with Catholicism; it was not with church councils; it was not with the Law of Constantine. It was already a practice among all churches outside the Land of Israel.

2. The Origin of the Sunday Sabbath

In determining the origin of the Sunday Sabbath, one must distinguish between viewing Sunday as a day of worship in contrast to Sunday as a Sabbath day. Historically, while Sunday was originally viewed as a day of worship, it was not considered a day of rest, nor was it considered a Sabbath day. Only with the church councils did Sunday begin to be viewed as a Sabbath.

As stated before, the church councils did not originate the Sunday worship; it was already the practice of the majority of churches. What the church councils did begin to do was to refer to Sunday as a "Sabbath." As church history developed, more and more Sabbath laws from the Old Testament were applied to Sunday. Today, people use terms like "Christian Sabbath" or "Sunday Sabbath." Biblically and technically, the concept of "Christian Sabbath" is just as wrong as "Jewish Sunday." There is no such thing as a Jewish Sunday, and there is no such thing as a Christian Sabbath. But because this has been so ingrained in Gentile church history, many believe that it is proper terminology.

For example, Charles Hodge, a famous systematic theologian, said that all Ten Commandments still apply, including the fourth commandment, the commandment on the Sabbath. Having made the claim that the Sabbath commandment still applies, he went on to say that the commandment now applies not to Saturday, but to Sunday. All of Charles Hodge's evidences for the mandatory Sabbath law are derived from the Old Testament. He even goes so far as to insist that the United States government should pass Sabbath laws requiring Sunday observance, even among unbelievers. While all of his arguments come from the Law of Moses, he ignores the fact that the Law of Moses specified that the Sabbath is the seventh day of the week, not the first day of the week.[13]

Even Dispensationalists, who should know better, often fall into the same trap. One famous Dispensationalist, Merrill Unger, for instance, wrote in his Unger's Bible Dictionary:

> The seventh day marks God's creative rest. On the first day Christ was unceasingly active. The seventh day commemorates a finished creation, the first day a finished redemption. In the present dispensation of grace, Sunday

---

[13] Hodge, Charles; *Systematic Theology, In Three Volumes*. (Grand Rapids, Michigan: Wm. B. Eerdmans Publishing Company, Reprinted, May 1997), Vol. III, pp. 321-348.

perpetuates the truth that one-seventh of one's time belongs to God. In every other particular, there is a contrast.[14]

Unger wrote that as the Sabbath commemorates God's creation rest, the first day speaks of God's resurrection rest. He feels that Sunday is now the day, which is to be set aside for God, although there is no New Testament command to do so.

The catalog of the Criswell Bible College and Graduate School of the Bible makes the same mistake:

> The first day of the week is the Lord's Day. It is a Christian institution for regular observance. It commemorates the resurrection of Christ from the dead and should include exercises of worship and spiritual devotion, both public and private. Activities on the Lord's Day should be commensurate with the Christian's conscience under the Lordship of Jesus Christ.[15]

In this catalog, the students are taught that Sunday is now the "Lord's Day." They have made it a day of rest, something the Bible itself never did.

The elders of a famous church in California, Grace Community Church, made the same mistake:

> To a Jew, the Old Testament taught them, *So you shall keep my statutes and my judgments by which a man may live if he does them* (Leviticus 18:5). The Jew was taught that if he was obedient he would get his reward at the end. In commenting on the fifth commandment in Exodus 20:12, the apostle Paul says that honoring one's father and mother was the first commandment with a promise of more days at the end of one's life. This was also how the Jew viewed the Sabbath. He lived six days in obedience to God and was rewarded on the

---

[14] Merrill F. Unger, "Sabbath," in *The New Unger's Bible Dictionary* (ed. R. K. Harrison; Chicago: Moody Publishers, 1988/2006).
[15] Criswell Bible College Catalog. Volume 39, p. 27. Dallas, TX. 2013.

seventh day with a day of rest. However, for the Christian, God has already rewarded him. There is, therefore, now no condemnation to those who are in Christ Jesus. Thus we have the Lord's Day at the beginning of the week, and live out our lives the rest of the week. The injunction to observe the Sabbath is the only one of the Ten Commandments that does not have a counterpart somewhere in the New Testament. The insistence of all Christians, both Jews and Gentiles in the early church, to observe the Lord's Day, Sunday rather than the Sabbath, Saturday, is proof positive that all Christians perceive the day change as more than just a matter of preference, convenience or sentimentality.

All of these quotations make some radical assumptions, which the authors do not even try to prove one way or the other. In particular, they do not even try to prove that somehow Sunday is the New Testament day of worship, that Sunday is a mandatory day of worship, whether they call it the Sabbath or the Lord's Day. This is a product of church history, not a product of New Testament teaching. The product of church history and church councils was to begin referring to Sunday as a Sabbath, as the Lord's Day, and as a "day of rest." While certainly Sunday worship did begin with the New Testament, the concept of a Sunday Sabbath did not.

3. The Beginning of the Sunday Service

By the end of the first and the beginning of the second century, the Sunday service was the practice of all the churches outside of Israel. That the Sunday service originated in the first century is seen in two ways. First, it was already found among the Pauline churches. We see this in Acts 20:7 with the Church of Troas, and in I Corinthians 16:2 with the Church of Corinth.

Second, it did not begin strictly with the Gentile churches that were established by Paul, but it had an even earlier origin. It began with the Jewish believers in the Land. Actually, Jewish believers in the Land of Israel began holding services on the first day of the week. Because they continued to go to the Temple or to synagogue on the Sabbath, they also wanted to gather among themselves as Jewish believers; so another time was required for believers to worship. The first day of the week was chosen out of convenience. Keep in mind that with the Jewish people, the first day of the week was not only Sunday morning, but also it included Saturday night. On Saturday night, the Jewish believers gathered among themselves. An early church father, Eusebius, in his book on the history of the church, points out that there were two different groups of Ebionites, one segment of the messianic movement in the first four centuries in the Land of Israel. One group kept the Sabbath only, while the other group kept both the Sabbath and Sunday.

However, while it was the Jewish believers who were meeting on the first day of the week, keep in mind these four things. First, they did not call that day a "Sabbath." Second, they did not make it a day of rest. Third, they did not transfer the Sabbath laws to Sunday. And fourth, for them, it was only a day of worship, not a day of rest and not a Sabbath day.

4. The Basis of Sunday Worship

The origin of the Sunday service was based on six events which occurred on that day. The first event was the Resurrection of the Messiah (Mat. 28:1; Mk. 16:2; Lk. 24:1; Jn. 20:1). The second event was that He appeared to the ten disciples on a Sunday (Jn. 20:19). The third event was that He appeared to the eleven disciples a week later, also on a Sunday (Jn. 20:26). The fourth event was that the birthday of the Church occurred on the first day of the week, a deduction which can be made by comparing Acts 2:1-4 with Lev. 23:15-16. The fifth event was that it was the time when the Church of Troas gathered together (Acts 20:7). And the sixth event was that it was the time that the offering was to be set aside (I Cor. 16:2).

5. The Evidence from the *Talmud*

The Jewish *Talmud* makes a clear statement showing that it was Jewish believers who began worship on the first day of the week. The *talmudic* statement reads as follows:

> On the eve of the Sabbath they did not fast out of respect to the sabbath still less did they do so on the sabbath itself. But why did they not fast on the day after the sabbath? Rabbi Yochanan says because of the Nazarenes (Babylonian *Taanit* 27b).

The term "Nazarenes" was an early term for Jewish believers, used even as early as the Book of Acts. In Judaism, out of respect for the Sabbath, the Jews feast on the Sabbath; they do not fast on the Sabbath. Furthermore, out of respect for the Sabbath, they do not fast on the day before the Sabbath either. The question that this rabbinical quote asked is, "Why do they not fast on the day after the Sabbath, which is Sunday?" The answer is, "To avoid showing any respect for the day regarded as special by the Nazarenes." If we keep in mind the meaning of the word "Nazarenes," it becomes obvious that Jewish believers were meeting for their worship services on the first day of the week.

B. The First Day of the Week

1. The Names

The first day of the week is never called three things: It is never called "the Sabbath," Scripture never calls it "Sunday", and it is never called "the Lord's Day." The biblical name for this day is always *the first day of the week*. This is in keeping with the Hebrew designation of that day.

2. The Lord's Day

The question is raised: Is it not called "the Lord's Day" in Revelation 1:10? The answer is that Revelation 1:10 does mention *the Lord's day*, but this is not a reference to Sunday. In the Greek text, the term *Lord* is not a noun, but it is an adjective. Literally, it means "a lordy day." Technically, it is not referring to any day of the week. It simply refers to a day when John was enraptured by prophetic and divine ecstasy. On that day, he fell under the Holy Spirit's control and was given prophetic inspiration. For John, it was indeed "a lordy day". The text does not state which day of the week it was. That "lordy day" may have been Sunday; it could have been Tuesday or Thursday. Even Revelation 1:10 does not use the term *the Lord's day* as a reference to Sunday.

3. Acts 20:7-8 and 11

⁷And upon the first day of the week, when we were gathered together to break bread, Paul discoursed with them, intending to depart on the morrow; and prolonged his speech until midnight. ⁸And there were many lights in the upper chamber where we were gathered together.

***

¹¹And when he was gone up, and had broken the bread, and eaten, and had talked with them a long while, even till break of day, so he departed.

What is clear from these passages is that the Church of Troas met on *the first day of the week*. It should not be presupposed that this meant Sunday morning, as is customary today. In fact, the Church of Troas was meeting on *the first day of the week*, but it was Saturday night. As of sundown Saturday, the Sabbath ends and so the seventh day of the week comes to an end. What begins after sundown Saturday is *the first day of the week*.

Earlier, a statement was quoted that was made by Grace Community Church in California and how they applied the Sabbath day of rest concept and worship concept to Sunday. In my response, I wrote:

> Furthermore, your quotation of Acts 20:7 as proving a Sunday observance is not really true. The passage does say the first day of the week. But you are ignoring that for Jews the first day of the week happened to be sundown Saturday until sundown Sunday and did not begin with the midnight hour between Saturday and Sunday. The Jewish believers did not meet Sunday morning, as the Grace Community Church has chosen to do, and you have the freedom to do so, but met Saturday night. The meeting referred to in Acts 20:7 occurred on a Saturday night and not on a Sunday morning. A careful exegesis of verse 7 will clearly bring that point out. The verse says that on the first day of the week, when they were gathered to break bread, Paul began talking to them. The verse states that the church got together on the first day of the week, which, for Paul as well as for all Jews, begins sundown Saturday. The very next phrase states he was intending to depart the next day. The next day would have been the Gentile Sunday. He would have been traveling on Sunday morning rather than worshipping on Sunday morning. The proof of it

all is in the final phrase of verse 7, that he prolonged his message until midnight. This makes perfect sense if it is realized that the meeting of the church occurred Saturday night and not Sunday morning. If Grace Community wishes to believe that the meeting of Acts 20:7 occurred Sunday morning at 11:00 a.m. they would have to claim that Paul preached for thirteen straight hours, until midnight on Sunday. That would certainly make the whole passage totally nonsensical. The simple exegesis of Acts 20:7 is that the church of Troas met on the first day of the week, Saturday night after sundown, and Paul was planning to leave the city the next morning, or Sunday morning, because the service started at night. Because of other elements involved in the worship Paul began preaching and continued to preach and was already going past midnight. The fact that the church was meeting at night and not in the morning becomes rather evident in two ways. First, that Paul preached until midnight and second, that in verse 8 it was necessary to have lit lamps in the upper room where they were gathered. Those messianic congregations which insist on a Friday night or Saturday morning worship are wrong if they make it a requirement. If they merely make it optional they have the total freedom to do so. Those who insist on absolutely required Sunday worship are equally wrong because they have no biblical validity. If Grace Community Church wishes to use Acts 20:7 as a rule of thumb then they will have to insist on a Saturday night worship, not on a Sunday morning worship. The clear teaching of the New Testament is that in this dispensation of grace there is no particular day that is obligatory to be set aside. There is freedom in the Lord in the matter. Therefore, let each individual congregation make its own choice on the matter. To claim, as the paper does, that the insistence of all Christians, both Jew and Gentiles, in the early church to observe the Lord's Day, Sunday, rather than the Sabbath, Saturday, is proof positive that all Christians perceived that day change is more than just a matter of preference, convenience or sentimentality, is frankly false in several perspectives. It is first of all historically false in that the historical records of

Jewish Christianity in the land for the first four centuries show that the Jewish believers as a rule met together on Saturday night and not on Sunday. It is also theologically untrue because, first of all, Sunday is never referred to as the Lord's Day, nor is there any so-called proof positive that the day of worship was changed.

Getting back to the issue of the Church of Troas, it should again be pointed out clearly that the believers did meet on the first day of the week, but it was Saturday night, not Sunday morning. Furthermore, the observation of the first day of the week did not begin with Gentile believers, but with Jewish believers.

This has been the conclusion of some Gentile biblical scholars as well. This is also the conclusion of the authors of *From Sabbath to Lord's Day*. Max Turner, in his article quoted earlier, also states:

> We must conclude that it is barely imaginable that first-day Sabbath observance commenced before the Jerusalem Council. Nor can we stop there; we must go on to maintain that first-day Sabbath observance cannot easily be understood as a phenomenon of the apostolic age or of the apostolic authority at all . . . If an apostolic decision was made after the council on so important a matter as this, it would have been an easy decision to reach and it would inevitably have left its mark in the epistles and in Acts. But as we have seen, Acts is silent on the issue and Paul's handling of the controversies involving the Law and the Sabbath makes it difficult to believe that he knew of any Sabbath transference theology.[16]

Turner makes the point that, while *the first day of the week* was observed by the Jewish believers even within the Land, they did not view it as a Sabbath nor were they practicing "transference theology" by applying Sabbath laws to Sunday. The Jewish believers did meet on the first day of the week, but did not make it a Sabbath or a day of rest or transfer Sabbath laws to Sunday.

---

[16] Turner, "The Sabbath, Sunday, and the Law in Luke/Acts," 135-6.

These Gentile scholars clearly point out that historical records show no evidence of a Sunday observance being viewed as a Sabbath. Surely they did meet on Sunday, but they did not make it a Sabbath. The same work points out that, while the first day of the week was observed by Jewish believers even within the Land, they did not view it as a Sabbath nor were they practicing transference theology by applying Sabbath laws to Sunday.

4. Not Obligatory as a Day of Worship

While it was the Jewish believers' practice to meet on the first day of the week, nowhere in the Scriptures is the first day of the week made an obligatory day of worship; there is no command to meet on the first day of the week. It is not wrong for the local congregation to meet on the first day of the week, but it is not mandatory either.

5. The Status of Sunday

In most of the western world, Sunday has become a convenient day of worship. However, it cannot be imposed. As de Lacey further states:

> Paul's contribution to our quest, then, is limited but of significance. While he forbids us from stating that Christians may not observe Sunday as the Christian day par excellence, he also forbids us from imposing such observance as a duty upon our fellow believers. Since, at least in much of the world, Sunday is allowed to the majority of us as a day of rest and a day suitable for worship, we may surely gratefully receive it as such; but our study of Paul forbids us from erecting any theological edifice upon this convenient, but fortuitous fact.[17]

6. The Freedom to Choose

If a Jewish believer chooses to observe the Sabbath, he is free to do so, whether he observes it as a day of rest or a day of worship. If a Jewish congregation chooses to have its meeting on Saturday, it is also free to do so. However, it is forbidden to impose a mandatory Sabbath observance,

---

[17] De Lacey, "The Sabbath/Sunday Question," 185-6.

individually or corporately, just as it is forbidden to mandate a Sunday observance, individually or corporately.

7. The Conclusion

In conclusion, we quote again from de Lacey:

> It is not unreasonable to suppose that Sunday was seen at an early stage as an appropriate day for a Christian feast, and no doubt every Christian feast was at least in part a Eucharist. Nothing that we have seen in Paul's writings could lead us to suppose that he would deny the appropriateness of a meeting for worship and Eucharist on Sunday, whether or not he or the churches ever in fact contemplated such a practice. Some contemporary writers, however, wish to go further than this, in claiming that Sunday is the Christian Sabbath, and that its observance is therefore a fulfillment of the fourth commandment. We have already seen enough to realize what short shrift this approach would have received from Paul. Not only is he opposed to the reestablishment of the Decalogue as a law for the Christian life, but he is also quite happy to allow the seventh-day Sabbath to be observed—a position quite incompatible with any identification of Sunday as the Christian Sabbath.[18]

---

[18] De Lacey, "The Sabbath/Sunday Question," 185.

IX. THE SABBATH AND SUNDAY: SUMMARY AND CONCLUSIONS

Theologians have had their share of difficulties developing the proper doctrine about the Sabbath. The Sabbath was the sign, seal, and token of the Mosaic Covenant. As long as that covenant was in effect, the Sabbath Law was mandatory. Dispensationalism teaches that since the Law of Moses has been rendered inoperative, the Sabbath command no longer applies. Covenant Theologians with their insistence that the Law of Moses is still in effect also insist that the Sabbath law applies. However, they totally ignore exactly what Moses wrote about how to keep the Sabbath, and they even change the day of the week, which the Law of Moses does not allow. The Jewish believers who also insist on mandatory Sabbath keeping and somewhat inconsistently base their conviction on the Law of Moses at least retain it with the seventh day of the week.

The apologetics used for mandatory Sabbath-keeping are almost exclusively based upon the Old Testament for obvious reasons: There is no New Testament command for believers in general or Jewish believers in particular to keep the Sabbath. The claim that Sabbath observance is part of the New Covenant is nowhere supported by the New Covenant Scriptures themselves. In fact, if anything, they would teach the opposite.

But even during the Old Testament period, Sabbath observance underwent changes. During the period between Adam and Moses, there is no record of the observance of the Sabbath. The Book of Job, which took place during this period, never mentions the Sabbath.

During the period from Moses to *Yeshua*, the Sabbath was to be observed. The first mention of the Sabbath is in Exodus 16:23 and 29-30. In Exodus 20:10-11, it is embodied in the Ten Commandments. Nehemiah 9:14 specifies that the Sabbath began with Moses. Between Moses and *Yeshua*, the Sabbath was obligatory for Jews, not for Gentiles. In Exodus 31:12-17, it was *a sign* between God and Israel. In Deuteronomy 5:15, it was based upon the Exodus experience. In

Ezekiel 20:12 and 20, it was *a sign* between God and Israel. Finally, there was a prophecy of a future cessation of the Sabbath in Hosea 2:11.

In the present age, Saturday is still the Sabbath, but it is no longer obligatory. The Sabbath is mentioned nine times in the Book of Acts, but never in connection with the worship of the local gathering of believers. There is no mandatory Sabbath-keeping for today (Rom. 14:5; Gal. 4:9-10; Col. 2:16-17).

Finally it can be noted that in the Messianic Kingdom, the Millennium, the Sabbath will be observed, and it will be mandatory (Is. 66:23; Ezek. 46:1).

Concerning Sunday worship, there are three observations. First, regarding the name of this day, it is never called the "Sabbath" and it is never called the "Lord's Day" in the Bible. It is always referred to as *the first day of the week*.

Second, the observance of Sunday worship was based upon the Resurrection and other events which occurred on that day.

Third, Sunday observance is not mandatory. It is the choice of most local congregations today, but any congregation, at any time, is free to choose to meet on another day.

X. THE SABBATICAL YEAR

The next two chapters of our study do not deal with the Sabbath day per se; nevertheless, they are relevant to the study of the Sabbath. The first category is the Sabbatical Year.

A. The Passages

There are nine passages of Scripture that mention the Sabbatical Year.

1. Exodus 23:10-11

The first passage deals with the Sabbatical Year proper.

[10] And six years you shall sow your land, and shall gather in the increase thereof: [11] but the seventh year you shall let it rest and lie fallow; that the poor of your people may eat: and what they leave the beast of the field shall eat. In like manner you shall deal with your vineyard, and with your oliveyard.

2. Leviticus 25:1-7

The second passage deals with the laws of the Sabbatical Year.

[1] And Jehovah spoke unto Moses in mount Sinai, saying, [2] Speak unto the children of Israel, and say unto them, When ye come into the land which I give you, then shall the land keep a sabbath unto Jehovah. [3] Six years you shall sow your field, and six years you shall prune your vineyard, and gather in the fruits thereof; [4] but in the seventh year shall be a sabbath of solemn rest for the land, a sabbath unto Jehovah: you shall neither sow your field, nor prune your vineyard. [5] That which grows of itself of your harvest you shall not reap, and the grapes of your undressed vine you shall not gather: it shall be a year of solemn rest for the land. [6] And the sabbath of the land shall be for food for you; for you, and for your servant and for your maid, and for your hired servant and for your stranger,

who sojourn with you. ⁷And for your cattle, and for the beasts that are in your land, shall all the increase thereof be for food.

Verse 1 introduces the subject with God speaking to Moses at Mount Sinai, where he received this command.

Verse 2 deals with the Sabbath for the land. Specifically, He addressed the children of Israel, that it is a law for them, not for the Gentiles. The timing when this law went into effect was only upon entrance into the Land of Israel. The fact is that man is to keep a weekly Sabbath, but the land is to keep a yearly Sabbath.

Verse 3 deals with the six years, while verses 4-7 spell out what they must do on the seventh year. In verse 4a, it is a sabbatical rest. He calls the Sabbatical Year by two names: first, *a sabbath of solemn rest for the land*; and second, *a sabbath unto Jehovah.* Verse 4b lists two prohibitions: first, *neither sow your field*; and second, *nor prune your vineyard.* Verse 5 mentions what they must do concerning the things which grow of themselves. There were two more prohibitions: First, *That which grows of itself of your harvest you shall not reap*; and second, *the grapes of your undressed vine you shall not gather.* These things, which would grow on their own accord during the Sabbatical Year, must be left alone. The reason is: *it shall be a year of solemn rest for the land.*

What are they to eat for the Sabbatical Year? He deals with this in verses 6-7. Verse 6 deals with man, and verse 7 deals with the animals. In other words, as the land produces on its own accord, they may pick, as they need to eat; furthermore, God will make the extra provisions of the previous years to be eaten.

3. Leviticus 25:18-22

The third passage is a promise of blessing on the sixth year.

¹⁸Wherefore ye shall do my statutes, and keep mine ordinances and do them; and ye shall dwell in the land in safety. ¹⁹And the land shall yield its fruit, and ye shall eat your fill, and dwell therein in safety. ²⁰And if ye shall say, What shall we eat the seventh year? behold, we shall not sow, nor gather in our increase; ²¹then I will command my blessing upon you in the sixth year, and it shall bring forth fruit for the three years. ²²And ye shall sow the eighth year, and eat of the fruits, the old store; until the ninth year, until its fruits come in, ye shall eat the old store.

In verse 18, there is the admonition to keep the commandments of God in order to dwell safely in the Land.

Verse 19 tells them what the results will be: The land will produce, and they will eat to the full. Furthermore, they will dwell in the Land safely.

Verses 20-21 raise a possible concern and a promise of provision.

In verse 22, the result will be that the produce of the sixth year will last for three years: It will last for the sixth year, when there is both sowing and reaping; it will last for the Sabbatical Year, when there is neither sowing nor reaping; it will also last for the eighth year, when there is sowing, but no reaping as yet. In the sixth year, God will provide enough to last *until the ninth year*, until there is the reaping of that which was sown in the eighth year.

4. Leviticus 26:34-35 and 43a

The fourth passage is a prophecy of punishment for failure to keep the Sabbatical Year.

³⁴Then shall the land enjoy its sabbaths, as long as it lies desolate, and ye are in your enemies' land; even then shall the land rest, and enjoy its sabbaths. ³⁵As long as it lies desolate it shall have rest, even the rest which it had not in your sabbaths, when ye dwelt upon it.

* * *

⁴³ᵃThe land also shall be left by them, and shall enjoy its sabbaths, while it lies desolate without them: . . .

This prophecy was fulfilled during the Babylonian Captivity. Verse 34 states: *Then shall the land enjoy its sabbaths*, when the Jews are forced into exile and the land lies desolate.

5. Deuteronomy 15:1-11

The fifth passage deals with the Sabbatical Year as the year of release from all debts. Verses 1-2 state:

> *¹At the end of every seven years you shall make a release. ²And this is the manner of the release: every creditor shall release that which he hath lent unto his neighbor; he shall not exact it of his neighbor and his brother;* [the reason being] *because Jehovah's release hath been proclaimed.*

In verse 3, he points out the distinction:

> *Of a foreigner* [a Gentile] *you may exact it: but whatsoever of yours is with your brother your hand shall release.*

In verses 4-6, he spells out blessings for obedience. In verse 4, there shall be no poor in the Land; in verse 5, the condition is obedience. In verse 6, Israel will *lend unto many nations, but you shall not borrow.*

In verses 7-8, meanwhile, they must be willing to lend to the poor.

In verse 9, they are not to use the coming of the Sabbatical Year as an excuse not to lend:

> *Beware that there be not a base thought in your heart, saying, The seventh year, the year of release, is at hand;* [then commit the sin] *and your eye be evil against your poor brother, and you give him nought;* [the result will be] *and he cry unto Jehovah against you, and it be sin unto you.*

In verse 10, there is the promise of blessing for obedience; then comes the command in verse 11 to lend to the poor and not to use the coming Sabbatical Year as an excuse not to do so.

6. Deuteronomy 31:9-13

The sixth passage deals with the reading of the Law during the Sabbatical Year. In verse 9, the Law is to be delivered to the Levites *and unto all the elders of Israel.*

Verses 10-11 mention what they must do on the Feast of Tabernacles when that feast falls on the Sabbatical Year:

> *[10] And Moses commanded them, saying, At the end of every seven years, in the set time of the year of release, in the feast of tabernacles, [11] when all Israel is come to appear before Jehovah your God in the place which he shall chose, you shall read this law before all Israel in their hearing.*

The timing, in verse 10, is at the end of every seven years, at a specific time: *the feast of tabernacles.* Verse 11 gives the purpose and the occasion: *when all Israel is come to appear before Jehovah.* This was the normal procedure for the Feast of Tabernacles. They would gather together for this feast in the place that God was to choose, which eventually became Jerusalem. The reason for the gathering of the seventh year is so they would hear the public reading of the Law.

Verses 12-13 give the goal of the reading of the Law: first, so that all can *hear* the Law, in verse 12; and second, so all can *learn* the Law, in verse 13.

7. II Chronicles 36:21b

The seventh passage records the fulfillment of the prophecy of Moses that the Jews would go into exile and then the land would have its rest:

> *... to fulfil the word of Jehovah by the mouth of Jeremiah, until the land had enjoyed its sabbaths: for as long as it lay desolate it kept sabbath, to fulfil threescore and ten years.*

8. Nehemiah 8:18

The eighth passage deals with the reading of the Law in keeping with the command of what to do when the Feast of Tabernacles falls in the Sabbatical Year. The fact that they read the Law during this Feast of Tabernacles clearly showed that this was a Sabbatical Year.

> *Also day by day, from the first day unto the last day,* [Ezra] *read in the book of the law of God. And they kept the feast seven days; and on the eighth day was a solemn assembly, according unto the ordinance.*

9. Nehemiah 10:31

> *[31] and if the peoples of the land bring wares or any grain on the sabbath day to sell, that we would not buy of them on the sabbath, or on a holy day; and that we would forego the seventh year, and the exaction of every debt.*

The ninth passage records how the Jewish people made a commitment to keep the Sabbatical Year and that they *would forego the seventh year, and the exaction of every debt.*

B. Observations and Conclusions

Eight observations and conclusions can be made concerning the Scriptures which mention the Sabbatical Year. First, on the seventh year, the land had to be allowed to lie fallow. There was to be no sowing and no reaping. There were specific inclusions: all crops, the vineyards or all vine crops, olive trees, and all orchards.

Second, that which grows on its own during the Sabbatical Year is not to be pruned or gathered or reaped or stored. It is to serve as food for the owner and his household, for the poor and the stranger, and for both domesticated and wild animals.

Third, the law applies only in the Land of Israel.

Fourth, it is a Sabbath rest for the land.

Fifth, failure to keep the sabbatical rest for the land would result in exile. Seventy sabbatical years were missed and the result was the seventy years of Babylonian Captivity to make up for them.

Sixth, God did promise that the land would produce enough on the sixth year to provide for the next three years: the sixth year, when there was both sowing and reaping; the seventh year, the Sabbatical Year, when there is neither sowing or reaping; and the eighth year, when there is sowing but no reaping. The land would produce enough to help them survive for three years.

Seventh, it was also a year of release from all debts. This was true of fellow Jews, but not true of Gentiles; the Gentiles would still be required to pay off their debts. The coming of the Sabbatical Year, however, was not to be used as an excuse not to lend to the Jewish poor.

And eighth, at the Feast of Tabernacles in the Sabbatical Year, the Law of Moses was to be read publicly.

C. The Names

In the Scriptures, the Sabbatical Year has four names. The first name is *shabbat shabbaton*, which means "a Sabbath of solemn rest." It is used for the Sabbatical Year in Leviticus 25:4. The point of this first name is that the land was to have complete rest from all cultivation.

The second name is *shnat shabbaton*, which means "a year of solemn rest." It is used of the Sabbatical Year in Leviticus 25:5. The point of the second name is that the rest was to extend throughout the year.

The third name is *shnat hashmittah*, which means "the year of release." This name is found in Deuteronomy 15:1-2 and 9. The point of *shnat hashmittah* is that in this year all debts to the Jewish poor are to be remitted.

The fourth name is *shnat hasheva*, which means "the seventh year." This is the name found in Deuteronomy 15:9. The point of *shnat hasheva* is that the Sabbatical Year was to be observed every seventh year.

D. The Biblical Laws

The first biblical law is that the soil, vineyards, and olive groves were to have perfect rest (Ex. 23:10-11; Lev. 25:2-5).

The second biblical law is that the spontaneous growth of the fields and trees during the Sabbatical Year was for free use, not only by the owners, but also by the poor, the hirelings, the strangers, the servants, and cattle (Ex. 23:10-11; Lev. 25:2-5). Furthermore, God promised a fruitful year on the sixth year to make up for the Sabbatical Year (Lev. 25:20-21).

The third biblical law had to do with the remission of debts. Except for foreigners, there was to be full remission of debts (Deut. 15:1-4). This did not mean an entire renunciation of what was owed. It simply meant that one did not press for repayment during the Sabbatical Year. Furthermore, it did not preclude or forbid voluntary payment of debts, but it did forbid enforced liquidation. The point was that, during the Sabbatical Year, no poor man was to be oppressed by his Jewish brother.

The fourth biblical law applied to the Feast of Tabernacles in a Sabbatical Year. Whenever the Feast of Tabernacles fell in a Sabbatical Year, they were to read the Law of Moses to the people. The audience had to include men, women, children, and strangers, who were gathered in solemn assembly before the Sanctuary (Deut. 31:10-13).

E. Rabbinic Laws and Traditions

The rabbis added some rules and regulations and traditions beyond the Scriptures. Five of these will be mentioned.

The first rabbinic law or tradition is that the law concerning the Sabbatical Year was to promote the idea of a theocracy. One year in seven would be devoted to serving the Lord.

The second rabbinic law applied from the Feast of Trumpets to the Feast of Trumpets, from *Rosh Hashanah* to *Rosh Hashanah*. That was the original law. A bit later the rabbis added the prohibition against planting and sowing beginning thirty days before the Feast of Trumpets. Still later, they prohibited the sowing of grain even from Passover before the Feast of Trumpets. Furthermore, it was prohibited to plant trees from Pentecost before the Feast of Trumpets.

The third rabbinic law is that anything planted, wittingly or unwittingly, during the Sabbatical Year had to be uprooted.

The fourth rabbinic law or tradition is that there were three positive and six negative commandments concerning the Sabbatical Year. The three positive commandments are: The land was to lie fallow (Ex. 23:11). It was a Sabbath of solemn rest for the land (Lev. 25:4). And it was to be a year of release (Deut. 15:1-2). The first four of the negative commands are found in Leviticus 25:4-5. There was to be no sowing of fields, no pruning of vineyards, no reaping of that which grew of itself, and no gathering of grapes from undressed vines. The fifth negative command was that there was to be no exacting of loans of a neighbor (Deut. 15:2). And the sixth negative command was that there were to be no base thoughts concerning lending to the poor (Deut. 15:9).

The fifth rabbinic law and tradition had to do with the application of the law of the Sabbatical Year and involved two things. First, the agricultural facets of the sabbatical laws were limited to the Land of Israel. In other words, a Jew having a farm in a different country did not have to keep the Sabbatical Year. A second thing about the application of this law is that the remittance of debts was to be applicable both inside and outside the Land of Israel during the Sabbatical Year.

F. The Ramifications

There are three ramifications that can be pointed out about the Sabbatical Year, the first one being that the spirit of the Sabbatical Year was based upon the weekly Sabbath.

The second ramification was the central idea of the Sabbatical Year: God is the owner of the soil and the Land. By grace, Israel was allowed to live in the Land. They, and their time, belonged to God. Therefore, they should thank Him for their material blessings. The basis for this was Israel's being the Chosen People. God's will was to be applied even agriculturally; hence, the sabbatical law.

The third ramification is the intent of the Sabbatical Year. The intent was rooted in God's dealings with Israel, and it covered three areas: Economically, it meant rest for the land. Socially, it meant relief for the poor. Spiritually, it was a time of religious instruction which is the reason that the Law of Moses had to be read on this occasion.

G. The History of its Observance

The Sabbatical Year was not observed during the Old Testament period, from the conquest of the Land until the Babylonian Captivity (II Chr. 36:21).

It was observed during the Second Temple period (Neh. 10:32). It began on the first day of the civil year, which is the Feast of Trumpets. The land on which the trees were planted was not cultivated after Pentecost of the sixth year. The grain fields were not cultivated as of Passover of the seventh year. Both Alexander the Great and Julius Caesar exempted Jews from paying taxes on the Sabbatical Year for that reason. Tacitus, the Roman historian, said:

> For the seventh day they are said to have prescribed rest because the day ended their labors. In addition being allured by the lack of energy they also spent the seventh year in laziness.

While this is a criticism by a Gentile against the Jewish observance of the Sabbath, it is, nevertheless, historical evidence that the Jews did keep the Sabbatical Year during the Second Temple period (515 B.C.-A.D. 70).

Sabbath Year observance continued after A.D. 70, but the restrictions eased after the Bar Cochba revolt (A.D. 132-135).

XI. THE YEAR OF JUBILEE

The final major category, also related to the concept of the Sabbath, is the Year of Jubilee.

A. The Passages

There are five passages that deal with the Year of Jubilee.

1. Leviticus 25:8-55

The first passage is the most extensive one, and it gives some general directions concerning the Year of Jubilee. This passage can be subdivided into eight parts.

a. Leviticus 25:8-12

The first part deals with the fiftieth year. Verse 8 speaks of the forty-nine years. In verse 9, the Israelites were to make the proclamation to be announced by the blowing of the trumpet:

> *⁸And you shall number seven sabbaths of years unto you, seven times seven years; and there shall be unto you the days of seven sabbaths of years, even forty and nine years. ⁹Then shall you send abroad the loud trumpet on the tenth day of the seventh month; in the day of atonement shall ye send abroad the trumpet throughout your land.*

The date they are to blow the trumpet is *the tenth day of the seventh month*, which was also *the day of atonement*. This month is now known as the month of *Tishrei*. This is the month that begins the Jewish civil year. It marks the end of the forty-ninth year and the beginning of the fiftieth year insofar as the Year of Jubilee is concerned. The extent is: *throughout all your land.*

The Year of Jubilee is to be proclaimed as a year of liberty in verse 10:

> *And ye shall hallow the fiftieth year, and proclaim liberty throughout the land unto all the inhabitants thereof: it shall be a jubilee unto you; and ye shall return every man unto his possession, and ye shall return every man unto his family.*

The Year of Jubilee is to be the basis of a Sabbath rest for the Land as seen in verse 11:

> *A jubilee shall that fiftieth year be unto you: ye shall not sow, neither reap that which grows of itself in it, nor gather the grapes in it of the undressed vines.*

In verse 12, the Israelites were merely to eat that which grows of itself. Again, the basis is:

> *For it is a jubilee; it shall be holy unto you: ye shall eat the increase thereof out of the field.*

b. Leviticus 25:13-17

The second subdivision deals with the return of land possessions. Verse 13 states:

> *In this year of jubilee ye shall return every man unto his possession.*

In verse 14, no cheating was allowed:

> *And if you sell aught unto your neighbor, or buy of your neighbor's hand, ye shall not wrong one another.*

In verses 15-16, the Year of Jubilee was to be used as a basis for determining property values:

> [15] *According to the number of years after the jubilee you shall buy of your neighbor, and according unto the number of years of the crops he shall sell unto you.* [16] *According to the multitude of the years you shall increase the price thereof, and according to the fewness of the years you shall diminish the price of it; for the number of the crops does he sell unto you.*

In other words, because the property would have to be returned to its original family ownership in the Year of Jubilee, if it had to be sold, its value was based upon how many years were left before the next Year of Jubilee when it would be returned. The further away one was from the Year of Jubilee, the higher the property was valued. The closer it was to the Year of Jubilee, the more the value would decrease.

In verse 17, again there is an admonition against cheating:

And ye shall not wrong one another; but you shall fear your God: for I am Jehovah your God.

c. Leviticus 25:18-22

The third subdivision deals with the Sabbatical Year, which was discussed earlier.

d. Leviticus 25:23-28

The fourth subdivision deals with the redemption of the land in verses 23-24:

²³And the land shall not be sold in perpetuity; for the land is mine: for ye are strangers and sojourners with me. ²⁴And in all the land of your possession ye shall grant a redemption for the land.

In verses 25-28, Moses deals with the situation of the land being sold because of poverty. In verse 25, if the land was sold because of poverty, it could be redeemed by a "kinsman-redeemer." In verses 26-27, the seller could redeem it if he became rich. However, in verse 28, Moses deals with the Year of Jubilee:

But if he be not able to get it back for himself, then that which he has sold shall remain in the hand of him that has bought it until the year of jubilee: and in the jubilee it shall go out, and he shall return unto his possession.

e. Leviticus 25:29-34

The fifth subdivision deals with the redemption of a house. In verses 29-30, if a house is sold within a walled city then, in verse 29, it can be redeemed within one year. In verse 30, if it is not redeemed within the space of a full year, *then the house that is in the walled city shall be made sure in perpetuity to him that bought it, throughout his generations;* it will not go back to the original owner in the Year of Jubilee.

In verse 31, he deals with the issue of a house in an unwalled village:

> *But the houses of the villages which have no wall round about them shall be reckoned with the fields of the country: they may be redeemed, and they shall go out in the jubilee.*

They will certainly be returned to the original family ownership in the Year of Jubilee.

In verses 32-34, Moses deals with the special case of the Levites. In verse 32, a Levite can redeem his house in any village or city *at any time.* In verse 33, if it has not been redeemed, then it will be returned to him in the Year of Jubilee. In verse 34, the Levites' fields and pasturelands can never be sold, *for it is their perpetual possession.*

f. Leviticus 25:35-38

The sixth subdivision teaches that they are not to loan money to fellow Jews with interest.

g. Leviticus 25:39-46

The seventh subdivision deals with the release of slaves. In verse 39, a fellow Jew is never to be made into a bond-servant. In verse 40a, he is always to be treated as *a hired servant.* In verse 40b-41, he is to be released in the Year of Jubilee with his whole family. He is to return to his ancestral possessions. The reason is given in verses 42-43:

> [42]*For they are my servants, whom I brought forth out of the land of Egypt: they shall not be sold as bondmen.* [43]*You shall not rule over him with rigor, but shall fear your God.*

In verses 44-46, it is permissible to make bondmen of the Gentiles in verse 44, and their children in verse 45. But in verse 46, Jews are not allowed to be forcefully turned into bondmen.

h. Leviticus 25:47-55

The eighth subdivision deals with the case of a Jew sold into slavery to a Gentile. In verse 47, Moses deals with the possibility of such a selling. In verses 48-49, such a person could be redeemed by a kinsman-redeemer. In verses 50-52, the price of redemption is to be based on the number of years that are left before the Year of Jubilee. In verse 53, the slave is to be treated as a hired servant. In verse 54, if he is not redeemed, then he shall be freed in the Year of Jubilee with his family. The reason is in verse 55: all Jews are the servants of God.

2. Leviticus 27:16-25

The second passage has to do with the application of the Year of Jubilee law on lands which are dedicated to Jehovah.

> *[16] And if a man shall sanctify unto Jehovah part of the field of his possession, then your estimation shall be according to the sowing thereof: the sowing of a homer of barley shall be valued at fifty shekels of silver. [17] If he sanctify his field from the year of jubilee, according to your estimation it shall stand. [18] But if he sanctify his field after the jubilee, then the priest shall reckon unto him the money according to the years that remain unto the year of jubilee; and an abatement shall be made from your estimation. [19] And if he that sanctified the field will indeed redeem it, then he shall add the fifth part of the money of thy estimation unto it, and it shall be assured to him. [20] And if he will not redeem the field, or if he have sold the field to another man, it shall not be redeemed any more: [21] but the field, when it goes out in the jubilee, shall be holy unto Jehovah, as a field devoted; the possession thereof shall be the priest's. [22] And if he sanctify unto Jehovah a field which he has bought, which is not of the field of his possession; [23] then the priest shall reckon unto him the worth of your estimation unto the year of jubilee: and he shall give your estimation in that day, as a holy thing unto Jehovah. [24] In the year of jubilee the field shall return unto him of whom it was bought, even to him to whom the possession of the land belongs. 25 And all your estimations shall be according to the shekel of the sanctuary: twenty gerahs shall be the shekel.*

In verse 16, the Israelites are to estimate the value of a field which is dedicated to Jehovah. In verse 17, the estimation is based upon when the dedication came in relation to the Year of Jubilee. In verse 18, if the field was dedicated after the Year of Jubilee, then the estimation will be based on how many years are left before the next Year of Jubilee. In verse 19, if the donor wants to redeem it, then twenty percent of the value is to be added to the original price. In verse 20, if he does not redeem it, or it is sold to another man, it can no longer be redeemed. In verse 21, in the Year of Jubilee it is to return to the priest, *as a field devoted*. In verses 22-23, if a party who then donates it to the Lord buys a field, the value is to be determined by how many years are left before the next Year of Jubilee. In verse 24, in the Year of Jubilee it is to be returned to the original owner from whom it was bought. In verse 25, the legal currency to be used for such transactions is the *shekel*.

3. Numbers 36:4

The third passage states that in the Year of Jubilee the land cannot go to the ownership of one who was outside the tribe, for the land must stay within its own tribal territory.

> *And when the jubilee of the children of Israel shall be, then will their inheritance be added unto the inheritance of the tribe whereunto they shall belong: so will their inheritance be taken away from the inheritance of the tribe of our fathers.*

If intermarriage had taken place, the land must still remain within its own tribal territory.

4. Isaiah 61:2

The fourth passage gives the messianic implication of the Law of the Year of Jubilee:

> *. . . to proclaim the year of Jehovah's favor, and the day of vengeance of our God; to comfort all that mourn; . . .*

In the Mosaic Law, the Year of Jubilee was a year of favor, a year of special grace. Part of the Messiah's mission was to proclaim *the year of Jehovah's favor*. This was part of the message of the First Coming. This is stated to be such in Luke 4:17-19, which quotes this passage. What *Yeshua* declared was *the year of Jehovah's favor*, that the blessings of the Year of Jubilee were being fulfilled in His messianic mission.

5. Ezekiel 46:17

The fifth passage deals with the Year of Jubilee in the Messianic Kingdom.

> *But if he give of his inheritance a gift to one of his servants, it shall be his to the year of liberty; then it shall return to the prince; but as for his inheritance, it shall be for his sons.*

The verse states that if *the prince* gives a portion of his land to one of his servants as a gift, it is the servant's until the Year of Jubilee, and then it is to be returned to *the prince*. Based upon this passage, the Year of Jubilee will be observed in the Kingdom. The *prince* is the resurrected King David. The resurrected King David will be given his own private territory in the Messianic Kingdom. He may choose to give portions of the land to his servants in the Kingdom. However, in the Year of Jubilee, they will be returned to him.

6. Observations and Conclusions

The Year of Jubilee is to be observed every fifty years, from the end of the forty-ninth year until the beginning of the fifty-first year.

It was to be reckoned from *Yom Kippur* to *Yom Kippur*, from the Day of Atonement until the Day of Atonement. In Leviticus 23, the Day of Atonement fell in the seventh month, not in the first month. The Year of Jubilee was to be reckoned from the tenth day of the seventh month until the following tenth day of the seventh month.

The Year of Jubilee was to be announced by a trumpet. There was to be a blowing of a trumpet throughout the Land announcing the beginning of the Year of Jubilee.

It was to include a proclamation of liberty. It was a proclamation of liberty in two senses: First, it meant the release of all Jewish slaves with their families; and second, it meant liberty because it included a restoration of property.

The Year of Jubilee was a sabbatical rest for the land. That meant a total of two years of Sabbath rest for the land. The forty-ninth year was a Sabbatical Year, which meant it was a year of Sabbath rest for the land;

but the fiftieth year was the Year of Jubilee, and that, too, was to be a Sabbath rest for the land. In those cases, there was a continuous two-year period of Sabbath rest for the land.

Furthermore, the Year of Jubilee was used to determine the value of property. A house that was within a walled city would not be returned in the Year of Jubilee because there was no property attached to the house itself. A house in an unwalled village would be returned in the Year of Jubilee since it was attached to land and property. It was to be reckoned the same way as the land. In any case, a house of a Levite is to be returned in the Year of Jubilee, whether the house was in a walled city or in an unwalled village.

Furthermore, in the Year of Jubilee, the ownership of the land was not to go outside the tribe to which it originally belonged. It was to remain within the original tribal territory, regardless of whether or not intermarriage might have taken place.

The Year of Jubilee was symbolic of the ministry of the Messiah at His First Coming in that He proclaimed freedom from slavery to sin. It will be observed in the Messianic Kingdom. It will be one of those things that will be mandatory in the Messianic Kingdom.

B. The Names

There are three names for the Year of Jubilee. The first name is *shnat hayoveil*, which means "the Year of Jubilee." The English word "jubilee" comes from this Hebrew word *yoveil*. The Hebrew "y" tends to turn into the English "j." The word *yoveil* means "the blast," specifically, the blast of a trumpet, which is the horn of a ram. This is how it is used in Leviticus 25:9. It is called the Year of Jubilee because the blowing of a trumpet, the blast of a trumpet, and the blast of the ram's horn announce this year.

The second name for this feast is *the year of Jehovah's favor* (Is. 61:2). It is this name that emphasizes the messianic implications. The Hebrew word for *favor* is the same as the word for "grace." The Year of Jubilee was a manifestation of God's grace. Of course, *Yeshua* came to proclaim God's grace in a special way: The Law came by Moses, but *grace and truth came through Yeshua Messiah* (Jn. 1:17).

The third name is *the year of liberty* (Ezek. 46:17). It was called *the year of liberty* because it meant liberty from indebtedness, and it meant the release of the property that was now being returned to its original owners. The context is a millennial one, which also points out that this will be observed in the Messianic Kingdom.

C. The Biblical Laws

There are five specific biblical laws dealing with the Year of Jubilee. The first biblical law is that it was obligatory only after the Jews entered into the Land of Israel and had cultivated the soil for 49 years. That is why Leviticus 25:8 states that it is to be after *seven sabbaths of years*. Leviticus 25:10 points out that it is specifically the *fiftieth year*. Furthermore, it was to begin on the tenth day of the seventh month of the fiftieth year, the day of *Yom Kippur*, the Day of Atonement.

The second biblical law had to do with the manner of its observance: They were to sound a trumpet throughout the Land (Lev. 25:10). The sounding of this trumpet blast would distinguish the forty-ninth year from the Year of Jubilee. The fiftieth year was to be hallowed as the Year of Jubilee.

The third biblical law is that it meant a rest for the soil. There was to be no sowing, no reaping, and no gathering from unpruned vines (Lev. 25:11). In other words, all of the laws of the Sabbatical Year were also to apply in the Year of Jubilee.

The fourth biblical law is that it meant a reversion of land property, a returning of all land property (Lev. 25:10-34; 27:16-24). All lands that were sold were now to revert back to the original owners or their heirs. There was, however, one key exception. A house within a walled city was not to be returned to its original owner, because houses in walled cities could only be redeemed within the first year after selling. After that, it became the permanent possession of the buyer and was not to be returned in the Year of Jubilee (Lev. 25:29-30).

The fifth biblical law is that it meant the freeing of Jews (Lev. 25:29-35, 39) in three areas: First, it meant going from being owned to being hired (Lev. 25:40, 53); second, it meant remission of all debts; and third, all land property of debtors was freely returned (Lev. 25:10, 13).

D. Rabbinic Laws and Traditions

There are three rabbinic laws and traditions regarding the Year of Jubilee. The first rabbinic law and tradition is that the first Sabbatical Year came 21 years after the arrival into the Land, so the first Year of Jubilee came 43 years later. Why was the first Sabbatical Year the twenty-first year? Because it took seven years to conquer the Land and then it took seven more years to distribute the Land. During the first 14 years, the Jews in the Land were not working on the land. During the following seven years they worked the land, so the first Sabbatical Year took place in the twenty-first year after arriving into the Land. It took another 43 years after that before the first Year of Jubilee came. The first Year of Jubilee was practiced 64 years after entering the Land.

The second rabbinic law and tradition is that there were a total of seventeen Jubilees from the time they entered the Land until the time they left it.

A third tradition is that there is a rabbinic saying:

> The world will endure not less than eighty-five jubilees and on the last jubilee the Son of David will come.

In other words, the rabbis guaranteed that the world would last for a total of at least 85 Jubilees, eighty-five times fifty years. When the final Jubilee comes, it may not be the eighty-fifth Jubilee because they only say that it will last at least 85 Jubilees. It might last longer. But whenever the last Year of Jubilee comes, the Messiah will come. In this rabbinic tradition, the year that the Messiah will come will be the Year of Jubilee.

E. The Ramifications

We can isolate three ramifications of the Year of Jubilee. First, the Year of Jubilee was given to keep the original allotment and divisions of the land intact. This was based on the way the land was divided among the tribes under Joshua, and then among families within the tribes.

The second ramification concerns the basis for the Year of Jubilee. The first basis is the concept that God owns the Land (Lev. 25:23). The second basis is the concept of God's ownership of all Jews as servants (Lev. 25:55).

The third ramification of the Year of Jubilee pertains to its three features. The first feature concerns personal liberty, and there are two things to note: Liberty was proclaimed to all Israelites in bondage. All Jews who, for one reason or another, had to sell themselves into slavery were proclaimed free. Furthermore, personal liberty included Jewish slaves for whom the six years had not yet expired. Normally a Jewish slave would serve six years and then be released in the seventh year. However, the Year of Jubilee was applied to Jewish slaves for whom the six years have not expired. If the Jewish slave had been a slave for three years, and then came the Year of Jubilee, he was released anyway.

The second feature of the Year of Jubilee was the restitution of property and five things should be noted on this point. First, it meant the return of ancestral possessions to those compelled to sell them because of poverty. If land or houses had to be sold, the property would be returned eventually. Second, it applied to lands and houses outside of walled cities, but not to houses inside walled cities. However, it applied to houses of Levites both inside and outside of walled cities. Third, it was the means of fixing the value for real estate property based upon how close to or how far it was away from the next Year of Jubilee (Lev. 25:15-16, 25-28). Fourth, it excluded the possibility of selling land permanently, which was the point of the Year of Jubilee (Lev. 25:23-24). The same rule applied to houses outside walled cities (Lev. 25:23-24). The same rule applied to all houses owned by Levites (Lev. 25:31). And fifth, the value of a Jewish slave was based on the proximity to the Year of Jubilee (Lev. 25:47-54).

The third feature of the Year of Jubilee was the principle of the simple life which is seen in three ways: First, the Year of Jubilee meant a year of rest for the land, which would require a simple lifestyle. Second, the land was to remain fallow for the second year following a Sabbatical Year. This meant that there would be two years of no sowing or reaping

(Lev. 25:18-22). And third, they were to live on what the land produced during the sixth year. This would also require some rationing and the simple life; they had to learn to live within a limited means of production.

F. The History of its Observance

The history is simple. It is not known whether the Year of Jubilee was observed during the period from Joshua until the Babylonian Captivity, but the implication is that it was not observed. Since they failed to observe the Sabbatical Year, probably they also failed to observe the Year of Jubilee.

During the Second Temple period (515 B.C.-A.D. 70), which was after the Jews returned from Babylonian Captivity, they did observe the Sabbatical Year. However, the same Jewish sources point out that they did not observe the Year of Jubilee during the Second Temple period. The Jewish *Talmud* teaches:

> From the time that the tribes of Reuben and Gad and the half tribe of Manasseh were exiled, the jubilees were discontinued.

Furthermore, rabbinic writings basically state that it is no longer known exactly when the Year of Jubilee is to fall, and therefore, the timing will not be known until Messiah comes.

XII. THE PRINCIPLE OF FREEDOM

At the beginning of this study about the Sabbath, we raised the question what Jewish and Gentile believers should do with the Sabbath. The answer, as we have found out, is quite simple: The believer in Messiah is free from the Law of Moses. This means that he is free from the necessity of keeping any commandment of that system. But on the other hand, he is also free to keep parts of the Law of Moses if he so desires.

The biblical basis for this freedom to keep the Law can be seen in the actions of Paul, the greatest exponent of freedom from the Law. His vow in Acts 18:18 is based on Numbers 6:2, 5, 9, and 18. His desire to be in Jerusalem for Pentecost in Acts 20:16 is based on Deuteronomy 16:16. The strongest passage is Acts 21:17-26, where we see Paul, the apostle of freedom from the Law, himself keeping the Law:

> [17]*And when we were come to Jerusalem, the brethren received us gladly.* [18]*And the day following Paul went in with us unto James; and all the elders were present.* [19]*And when he had saluted them, he rehearsed one by one the things which God had wrought among the Gentiles through his ministry.* [20]*And they, when they heard it, glorified God; and they said unto him, You see, brother, how many thousands there are among the Jews of them that have believed; and they are all zealous for the law:* [21]*and they have been informed concerning you, that you teach all the Jews who are among the Gentiles to forsake Moses, telling them not to circumcise their children neither to walk after the customs.* [22]*What is it therefore? they will certainly hear that you are come.* [23]*Do therefore this that we say to you: We have four men that have a vow on them;* [24]*these take, and purify yourself with them, and be at charges for them, that they may shave their heads: and all shall know that there is no truth in the things whereof they have been informed concerning you; but that you yourself also walk*

orderly, keeping the law. ²⁵*But as touching the Gentiles that have believed, we wrote, giving judgment that they should keep themselves from things sacrificed to idols, and from blood, and from what is strangled, and from fornication.* ²⁶*Then Paul took the men, and the next day purifying himself with them went into the temple, declaring the fulfillment of the days of purification, until the offering was offered for every one of them.*

The believer is free from the Law, but he is also free to keep parts of it. Thus if a Jewish believer feels the need to keep the Sabbath, he is free to do so. The same is true for all the other commandments.

However, there are two dangers that must be avoided by the Jewish believer who volunteers to keep commandments of the Law of Moses. One danger is the idea that by doing so he is contributing to his own justification and sanctification. This is false and should be avoided. The second danger is in one's expecting others to keep the same commandments he has decided to keep. This is equally wrong and borders on legalism. The one who exercises his freedom to keep the Law must recognize and respect another's freedom not to keep it.

SCRIPTURE INDEX

Genesis

2	2, 9, 12, 13
2:2-3	9, 12, 17, 100, 101
2:23-25	10
12	9

Exodus

12:16	27
14:13	37
16	16
16:23	115
16:23-30	15, 16, 24
16:29	24, 32
16:29-30	115
20	24
20:8	2, 7
20:8-11	16, 17
20:10	11, 2, 34, 115
21:6	37
23:10-11	117, 123, 124
23:12	17
27:20	37
27:21	36
28:43	37
29:28	37
30:21	36, 37
31:12-17	18, 32, 34, 115
31:13	34, 36
31:15	34
31:16	34, 36
31:17	34, 36
34:21	19, 24
35:1-3	19, 24
35:2	34
40:15	36, 37

Leviticus

6:18	36, 37
6:22	36
7:34	37
7:36	36, 37
10:9	36, 37
10:15	37
16:31	19
16:34	37
19:3	20, 34
19:30	20, 34
23	133
23:2	28
23:3	20, 27, 28, 32, 34
23:4	20, 28
23:7-8	29
23:11	21
23:15-16	21, 107
23:21	29
23:24	29
23:27	29
23:32	21
23:35-36	29
23:37	30
23:38	22
24:3	36, 37
24:8	33, 37
24:9	36
25:1-7	117
25:2-5	123, 124
25:4-5	123, 125
25:5	123
25:8	135
25:8-12	127
25:8-55	127
25:9	134
25:10	135, 136
25:10-34	135
25:11	135
25:13	37, 136
25:13-17	128
25:15-16	137
25:18-22	118, 129, 138
25:20-21	124
25:23-24	137
25:23-28	129
25:25-28	137
25:29-30	136
25:29-34	129, 136
25:30	36
25:31	137
25:35-38	130
25:39	136
25:39-46	130
25:40	136

25:46	37	36:4	132	11:7	51
25:47-55	130, 138			11:9	51
25:53	136	**Deuteronomy**		16:18	52
25:55	137	5:12	7, 17		
26:2	22, 34	5:12-15	23	**I Chronicles**	
26:34-35	119	5:15	33, 34, 115	9:32	61, 67
26:43a	119	12:9	100	15:2	37
27:16-25	131, 135	15:1-2	123, 125	23:13	37, 67
		15:1-4	124	23:31	61, 67
Numbers		15:1-11	120	28:4	37
6:2	139	15:2	125		
6:5	139	15:9	123, 125	**II Chronicles**	
6:9	139	15:17	37	2:4	62, 67
6:18	139	18:5	37	7:16	37
10:8	36, 37	31:9-13	121	8:12-13	67
15:15	36, 37	31:10-13	124	8:13	62
15:32-36	22, 24			31:2-3	62, 67
18:8	37	**Joshua**		36:21	121, 126
18:11	37	3:4	92		
18:18	139	5:12	1	**Nehemiah**	
18:19	37			6:3	1
18:23	36, 37	**I Samuel**		8:18	121
19:10	37	1:22	37	9:14	63, 115
20:16	139	2:35	37	10:31	63, 67, 121
21:17-26	139	20:23	37	10:32	126
28:9-10	23, 33	27:12	37	10:33	63, 67
28:25	30	28:2	37	13:15-22	64, 67
28:26	31				
28:28	30	**II Kings**		**Psalm**	
29:1	31	4:23	51	92	65, 67
29:12	31	11:5	51		

Isaiah

1:13	52, 60
7:14	43
13:11	2
24:8	1
56:1-8	52, 60
58:13	53, 60
61:2	132, 135
66:23	53, 60, 116

Jeremiah

17:21	59
17:21-27	54, 60
31:31-34	41

Lamentations

1:7	66
2:6	66
5:14	2

Ezekiel

6:6	2
20:10-12	33
20:12	60, 116
20:12-24	55, 60
20:20	60, 116
22:8	56, 60
22:26	56, 60
23:38	56, 60
44:24	57, 60
45:17	57, 60
46:1	116
46:1-5	57, 60
46:12	58, 60
46:17	133, 135

Hosea

1:4	2
2:11	59, 60, 116

Amos

8:5	59, 60

Matthew

1:22-23	43
3:13-17	78
5:17-19	43, 45
11:28-30	100
12:1-8	45
12:1-14	100
12:3-4	80
12:5	80
12:6	81
12:7	81
12:8	81, 91
12:9-14	82
12:10	82
12:11-12	83
12:14	84
13:54-58	84
19:10-12	10
24:20	88
28:1	89, 107

Mark

1:9-11	78
1:21-28	71
2:23-28	45
2:25-26	80
2:27	10, 81, 91
2:28	81
3:1-6	82
3:4	83
3:5	83
3:6	84
6:1-6	84
15:42	88
16:1	90
16:2	107

Luke

3:21	78
4:16-30	71
4:17-19	132
4:31-37	72
6:1-5	45
6:5	81
6:6	82
6:6-11	82
6:9	83
6:10	83
6:11	84
13:10-17	86

14:1-6	87	20:11	109	5:3-4	98
23:54	89	21:20-24	95	5:14	98
23:56	89			6:13	98
24:1	107	**Romans**			
		7:1-6	38	**Ephesians**	
John		10:4	39	2:11-16	40
1:17	135	14:4-6a	97		
1:29	77	14:5	116	**Colossians**	
5:1-47	72			2:16-17	96, 116
5:30	100	**I Corinthians**			
7:21-24	85	7:1-7	10	**Hebrews**	
9:1-41	85	16:2	106, 107	3:7-4:13	99, 101
19:31	89			4:3-4	10, 12, 101
20:1	107	**II Corinthians**		4:9	100, 101
20:19	107	3:2-11	41	7:11-12	40, 41
20:26	107			7:18	40
		Galatians		7:19	39
Acts		2:16	39, 98	8:5	96
1:12	92	2:19-20	98	8:13	41
2:1-4	107	3:2	98	10:1	96
13:14	92	3:5	98	10:25	102
13:27	92	3:10-29	98		
13:42	92	3:19	39	**James**	
13:44	92	3:23-25	42	2:10	44
15:1-20	94	3:24	40		
15:21	92	3:24-25	40	**Revelation**	
16:13	92	3:25	40	1:10	108, 109
17:2	92	4:4-5	98	20:5	76
18:4	92	4:9-10	116	21:8	76
20:7	106, 107, 109, 110	4:10	98		
		4:21	98		
20:7-8	109				

BIBLIOGRAPHY

D. A. Carson, "Jesus and the Sabbath in the Four Gospels," in *From Sabbath to Lord's Day: A Biblical, Historical and Theological Investigation* (ed. D. A. Carson; Grand Rapids: Zondervan, 1982).

Lewis Sperry Chafer, Grace: An Exposition of God's Marvelous Love *(Nabu Press, 2010)*.

Criswell Bible College Catalog. Volume 39, p. 27. Dallas, TX. 2013

Harold H. P. Dressler, "The Sabbath in the Old Testament," in *From Sabbath to Lord's Day: A Biblical, Historical and Theological Investigation* (ed. D. A. Carson; Grand Rapids: Zondervan, 1982).

Charles Lee Feinberg, "The Sabbath and the Lord's Day," *Bibliotheca Sacra* Apr. (1938): 172-194.

Charles Hodge, *Systematic Theology, In Three Volumes*. (Grand Rapids, Michigan: Wm. B. Eerdmans Publishing Company, Reprinted, May 1997), Vol. III, pp. 321-348.

D. R. de Lacey, "The Sabbath/Sunday Question and the Law in the Pauline Corpus," in *From Sabbath to Lord's Day: A Biblical, Historical and Theological Investigation* (ed. D. A. Carson; Grand Rapids: Zondervan, 1982).

A. T. Lincoln, "From Sabbath to Lord's Day: A Biblical and Theological Perspective," in *From Sabbath to Lord's Day: A Biblical, Historical and Theological Investigation* (ed. D. A. Carson; Grand Rapids: Zondervan, 1982).

M. Max B. Turner, "The Sabbath, Sunday, and the Law in Luke/Acts," in *From Sabbath to Lord's Day: A Biblical, Historical and Theological Investigation* (ed. D. A. Carson; Grand Rapids: Zondervan, 1982).

Merrill F. Unger, "Sabbath," in *The New Unger's Bible Dictionary* (ed. R. K. Harrison; Chicago: Moody Publishers, 1988/2006).